October 26, 2009
Alexander Road,
Petaluma, CA.
Two Rock

FIREMAN

BY

GEORGE R. KREUSCHER,
LIEUTENANT, RETIRED F.D.N.Y.

To Bob H.,
God Bless America.
We will NEVER forget.
Best Wishes
George Kreuscher

WWW.FIREMAN-BOOK.COM

Copyright © 2008 by George R. Kreuscher

All rights reserved. No part of this book may be reproduced, stored in a retrieval system or transmitted in any form, or by any means (electronic, mechanical, photocopying, recording, or otherwise), without prior written permission of the author.

The scanning, uploading and distribution of this book via the Internet or via any other means without the permission of the author is illegal and punishable by law. Please purchase only authorized electronic editions, and do not participate in or encourage electronic piracy of copyrighted material. Your support of the author's rights is appreciated

International Standard Book Number: 978-0-9799175-0-9

Library of Congress Control Number: 2007935182

Printed in the United States of America

Dedication

To my wife Mary Lou, and our adult children, George, Brandt, Erika, Leif, and their families.

Donations

There has always been a bond between the military and the fire service. That bond was forged on September 11, 2001. A portion of the proceeds of this book will go to wounded warriors.

Acknowledgments

To Mary Lou, who always had faith that I would write this book and was so helpful to me in many ways. Proofreading, typing, and rereading again and again. Always cheerful and willing. My partner.

To Al Fuentes, my study mate for promotion in the FDNY, author of *American by Choice,* and a good friend whose advice in the publication of this book was so valuable.

The cover portrait, "Lieutenant Kreuscher," was painted from life by Jesse Gardner for his "Unsung Heroes" exhibit in 1993. Jesse appreciated the contribution of firefighters to society long before September 11, 2001. Jesse resides in Philadelphia, Pennsylvania, with his wife and child.

The back cover, "Reverence for Life," was painted by Jeanette Capriano in 1974 and is also a representation of Rescue 1, FDNY, in action. Jeanette did a whole series of paintings that depicted the many aspects of the Fire Service. Her whole series on the FDNY Probationary Firefighters School hangs on the walls of the Fire Academy at Randalls Island, as well as the painting of the Emerald Society Band, "Pipes and Drums." "Reverence for Life" is displayed on the wall of the back room at the quarters of Rescue Company 1, West 43rd Street, Manhattan.

My thanks to Shelly Sapyta, Elaine Lattanzi, Ryan Feasel, and Tim Snider at BookMasters, Inc.

Special thanks to Tom Monaster and Angela Troisi of the *New York Daily News.*

Contents

	Introduction	ix
Chapter 1	Leif's Phone Call	1
Chapter 2	Leif Reads the List of the Dead	7
Chapter 3	The World Trade Center Site—Ground Zero	11
Chapter 4	Leif's First Sight of Ground Zero	17
Chapter 5	Kathy's Letter	21
Chapter 6	The Ladies on the Roof	25
Chapter 7	Waldbaum's Supermarket—August 2, 1978	31
Chapter 8	The Rescue Company	39
Chapter 9	Fire at Macy's	43
Chapter 10	Connections	51
Chapter 11	September 1979—A Night with the Pope	55
Chapter 12	Attempt at a Diary—102 Truck	65
Chapter 13	Pete Cusumano: A Firefighter	69

Chapter 14	Boy in the Shaft	79
	Photo Section	83
Chapter 15	Ring Jobs and the Ring Job	103
Chapter 16	School Fire at Fifty-First Street and First Avenue	109
Chapter 17	Funerals and Memorials	113
Chapter 18	Things That Happen on Any Day	119
Chapter 19	Elevators	127
Chapter 20	Honor	133
Chapter 21	Another Phone Call	137
Chapter 22	Fire Ground	149
Chapter 23	Eleventh Floor Aerial Rescue	155
Chapter 24	Explosion at a Senior Citizen's Center	161
Chapter 25	Trains	163
Chapter 26	Diving—Blackwater	167
Chapter 27	The Movies	177
Chapter 28	The FDNY Chaplain	181
Chapter 29	Some of the Men	187
	Epilogue	205
	Appendix	211

Introduction

Like most kids growing up in a big city or for that matter anywhere, the fire department, which was usually the local firehouse with its shiny red apparatus in the doorway, caught my attention.

The area I grew up in, during the 1940s and 1950s, was on the boundary of Brooklyn and Queens, just about where Ridgewood, Bushwick, and East New York come together. These areas, up to the twentieth century, were vestiges of farm communities that grew together into an area of row flats, frame townhouses that looked like brownstones, and some private houses from its more rural times. It was a working-class to middle-class area and, at that time, a pretty good place to grow up—a German area with Irish, Italians, Poles, Russians, and English mixed in. I didn't see much of the fire department in those days because there weren't many fires or emergencies, but the few times I did were memorable.

Eldert Street was between Engine 252 on Central Avenue between Schaefer and Decatur streets and Ladder 112 on Madison Street between Wilson and Central avenues. My first recollection of Engine 252 was going by the open door in the late 1940s and early 1950s and seeing their Rolls-Royce of fire engines, the long-hooded roadster "Ahrens Fox." Its front-mounted piston pump stuck way out front, with a shiny chrome ball that was two feet across sitting on top. It filled the doorway and a kid's imagination. Later, I would come to appreciate these one thousand gallon per minute pumps. They were as powerful as they looked.

In the first grade in P.S. (Public School) 106, we visited the nearest firehouse, which was Ladder Company 112 on Madison Street. In those days, Ladder Company 112, like all ladder companies of New York, was called by the nineteenth-century term of Hook & Ladder 112. The firemen were quite impressive to us kids, because especially in truck companies (ladder companies are called trucks), the men were very big and cordial. They raised the aerial ladder, which was varnished wood, to the roof of the firehouse, climbed it, and then slid the pole for us—a visit never to be forgotten.

The two things I remember most about Hook & Ladder 112 was how big and sturdy-looking those tall firemen were and the shrieking sound the long-tiller, aerial truck made when turning onto Wilson Avenue from Madison Street seven blocks away. The bright red lights on either side of the roadster windshield were magnified by the high-pitched, shrill scream of the Buckeye Whistle that was blown off the engine exhaust manifold. It got people's attention more than sirens and air horns do today. The Buckeyes were removed sometime in the fifties because they burned out the exhaust valves on the truck engines.

All the ladder company trucks and pumper engines before the late fifties were roadsters, the cabs being open all year-round. The thinking was that the firemen had better visibility coming into a fire scene, enabling a faster size up of what they were going to be dealing with. Little thought was given to the comfort of the firemen riding these trucks. Eventually, all engines, with pumps and hose, and then ladder trucks were covered.

These impressions of childhood were enhanced by a couple of Sunday school teachers I had who were firemen. They were genial, fine men a kid would want to emulate.

One of my best friends while growing up was Larry Zimmermann, whose father, Bill, was a fireman for 34 years. Whenever I had dinner at their house as a kid, Mr. Zimmermann would tell us things that were unusual and sometimes tragic. But, mostly, his stories were of an extremely funny nature that would make us feel like we had missed something by not being there ourselves.

All these things made some kind of impression on me back then, though I had never given thought to being a fireman myself. Years later, Larry would become a fireman like his father. Another friend, Bill Holm, would get us both applications for the fire department test. On May 23, 1964, Bill Holm and I entered the FDNY. Only one out of ten candidates makes it.

From the first, our experiences at the Fire Academy on Roosevelt Island were not disappointing. The firemen and lieutenants who instructed us were a tough lot. These guys had been around and you could tell they were confident men. They were not easy on us and, as a matter of fact, kept pressure on us all the time. They were trying to prepare us for the extreme tension of encountering the unknown. Nothing could completely prepare us for fire coming out of windows with people hanging out or worse with people trapped inside.

Even though we knew that a fireman died in the line of duty on average every five weeks, we still felt a certain invincibility.

On September 11, 2001, that feeling was gone forever. Nothing would be the same and never in the history of the world was a fire department so deeply wounded. Although I had been retired for 6 years, I had served more than 31 years and responded to twenty-eight thousand alarms, with one-third of those being fires, one-third of them emergencies of every kind, and the remaining third false alarms. In the two battalions in which I spent 26 years, all the men working that day were killed with the exception of Engine Company 209 and my son Leif's company, Ladder 102. Dennis Cross, The Iron Cross, my friend of 30 years, was Leif's battalion chief in the 57th Battalion. As an acting deputy chief of the 11th Division, he would respond that morning and die there, along with the other 342 firefighters and officers. About 100 of these were friends and men I had worked with over the years in the FDNY. At least 16 sons of friends would die that day.

There are thousands of acts of heroism every year in the Fire Department New York. Bravery is so commonplace that good, brave men are banging into each other at jobs, fighting to get into the most awful places to rescue people in trouble and extinguish fire. Through all this usual bravery, there are some we call the great heroes that we all recognize as standouts. They are the bravest of the brave and many of them died that day along with the brave.

The impact of this attack on America was so devastating that it has caused some to say that since September 11, 2001 there are three Fire Departments. There is the Fire Department Pre 9/11, the Fire Department of 9/11, and the Fire Department of Post 9/11.

With all that happened in the first 136 years of the FDNY, extraordinary fires, loss of life to civilians and firemen, it was a more innocent time. When the 343 men died on 9/11, it was half the number of those who died in the previous 136 years. On that day, 9/11 brought the number of line-of-duty deaths to well over one thousand. This devastation and loss brought about the loss of innocence that the Post 9/11 Fire Department New York will have to live with, at least until the last of those who were there are gone and maybe it will never be regained.

With all the danger there was in the Pre 9/11 Fire Department, it had an innocence about it that has not existed since September 11, 2001.

Back in 1964, when I went on the Fire Department New York, there was no way I could have predicted the experience it would turn out to be.

CHAPTER 1

Leif's Phone Call

The phone rings in our bedroom. It's 6:10 in the morning. It is just about the time my wife, Mary Lou, and I usually get up on the ranch in northern California. It's our son Leif. Even though it's 9:10 in New York, it is an unusual time for a call this early in California. "Dad, did you see on the news what happened at the World Trade Center?" he asks softly. Then he says, "A plane hit the building." I'm half asleep yet, and I say, "Could be an accident." He says, "No. It was two planes." I run out to the TV room, which is surrounded by windows, looking out at what promises to be a lovely northern California day. The sun's just peeking over the hill east of our valley. I flip the TV on and see the plane coming in and hitting the South Tower. I cannot believe my eyes. I am fully awake now, Mary Lou is at my side now, and I get right back to Leif. He's been a firefighter in the Fire Department New York for the last five years.

"Leif, you'll probably be recalled." He says, "Yeah, Dad, I better go so I can call and find out what's happening." We will not talk to him again for the next couple of days. He was at home when he called us. I call back 10 minutes later and he's already gone. It's a full recall of all off-duty fire personnel. This lovely September morning on both coasts of the United States will turn out to be the worst day of all of our lives. For Leif, it is the beginning of a couple of weeks of horrific carnage and unspeakable deeds. He will never be the same again, but he will have the company of thousands.

I put the phone down and it rings again immediately. It is our oldest son, George. He is a former Marine and former firefighter with the Fire Department New York, and was badly burned in a molotov cocktail attack in a riotous situation up in Washington Heights, Manhattan. After being burned, with five years in the fire department, he worked five more years in Ladder Company 44 in the Bronx. He had to leave the job he loved due to the physical damage to his hands from the burns. He's accepted this with grace. "How are you doing, Dad?" He is also aware that we will know many of the firefighters lost this day. We already suspect who's behind this terrible, blindsiding attack. He growls into the phone as only a true fighting man can, "It's time to get medieval." I will never forget that low growl from our otherwise very civilized son.

Mary Lou and I stand together in this multi-windowed TV room, watching both towers of the city, which look like two candles belching volumes of ugly, black smoke from the top floors. The beauty of northern California outside is no comfort. Our eyes are glued to the TV screen.

With the aid of telephoto lenses, the TV cameras are picking up closer views of the upper floors of the towers. We see heat-wavering images of the desperate souls waving handkerchiefs or anything that will get the attention of rescuers who will never come. Some people are climbing outboard to escape the heat and smoke from the intense fire inside and below.

I am standing in front of a television on a ranch in northern California with my wife of 39 years, but our total focus is on those towers in New York. We cannot yet comprehend how someone or some group could bring something like this on innocent fellow human beings.

As I watch the TV screen, I know the drill. In September 1995, I retired from the Fire Department New York after 31 years of service. Sixteen of these years were spent in Rescue 1, which was the Manhattan Rescue. I'd been to thousands of fires and emergencies of every kind imaginable. Many were in high-rise buildings. There were many procedures for when to, and when not to, use elevators. Under the conditions that existed between 8:45 and 10:28 a.m. on September 11, 2001, most firefighters would have had to use the stairs, and many would prefer the stairs to elevators with something of this magnitude, no matter how awful or arduous that seems.

So, after all these years of experience in Manhattan, like many other firefighters, I know this drill in my sleep. The elevators are unusable, untenable, or limited. It's the stairs and it will take a long time to get to those in need. Many will be trapped above. The rescuers will risk everything to reach them. For some, it will never happen. I stand there mesmerized by what I see with my eyes. Inside those buildings, I can see the drill in my mind's eye. The firefighters are a steady stream of enginemen carrying hose and truckmen and rescue men with tools of every kind, Scott Air Paks, and extra bottles. They are going up one side of the stairs, the survivors, fortunate civilians, are coming down the other side. My mind's picture is one of order. The civilians are civilized, decent people, the fire department firefighters are focused on the job above. People are in trouble and no matter that there's never been anything quite this calamitous in the world, like soldiers going toward the sound of gunfire, the firefighters are heading up to people in trouble.

Mary Lou and I stand facing the television screen, three thousand miles from New York. Like millions of other Americans on this day, our whole attention is on those towers. My mind is dulled and racing at the same time. Like many, I already know this is going to be a terrible day. My thoughts, of course, are with the violated innocents, but I am in those stairwells with those brave firefighters. They are trudging up those stairs, each carrying a hundred pounds of gear. They are hardly looking at those coming down. One step after the other, they are moving up to God knows what. Bathed in sweat, they are almost on automatic. After responding to twenty-eight thousand alarms in my own time, I cannot imagine what these men are ultimately getting into.

The news people on the TV are aghast, describing what they are seeing. I hear the sounds of the air horns and sirens from all those fire trucks and emergency responders converging on the World Trade Center. There are now reports of people jumping from the upper floors and deep down I know many must be trapped above.

A strange thing happens to me standing there. Time is compressed, unlike what happened years ago at a nasty fire on Bank and West streets. We of Rescue 1 were moving up the rear fire escape, removing tin from the rear windows, venting a full-blown, multiple-alarm fire. We were mounting the steps to the fourth-floor landing, when all six floors collapsed into the cellar in a fraction of a second. Debris was blowing out the windows like a blast from a shotgun. We were running for our lives, trying to get away from the windows to escape the debris of the floors snapping by from above, which had the potential to kill instantly. I can still see John McAllister's helmet next to me, turning from side to side in slow motion. I was outboard, sliding the frame that normally holds the drop ladder up; the ladder is down. The building was shaking violently and this was the closest I'd ever been to a building in collapse; if the rear wall had fallen outward, I would surely already have been dead. As I slid, the building shook, and I thought, "Is this it? Is this where I die?" on a beautiful sunny, late Sunday afternoon. I made it to the drop ladder, sliding the rails submariner-style, which I had never done before. I made it to the rear yard, looked up and saw the last of the rescue guys, including McAllister, climbing from the fire escape landing to the building next door. The collapse of all six floors took half a second and left us black as coal miners. My flight to get away from the third-floor windows and sliding into the rear yard took, at the most, two seconds. Yet, I can remember almost every detail over a period of time that seemed like minutes.

On September 11, 2001, the time between 9:05 and 10:00 a.m. is a blur and compressed. At 10:00, the news people scream that the building (the South Tower) has collapsed. From this point until 10:28, when the North Tower collapses, I cannot account for the time, except that I'm standing transfixed. There seems almost no time between the South Tower's collapse and when the North Tower collapses twenty-eight minutes later. The collapse of the second tower brings me to my knees in tears, grief, and prayer. My wife is in tears and tries to comfort me: "Oh, those beautiful men."

CHAPTER 2

Leif Reads the List of the Dead

Mary Lou and I are numb. We are far away and alone, except for each other. This ranch we love is a lonely place for us this morning. I know there will be hundreds dead from the fire department alone, and I will know many of them. The only thing we can think to do at this moment is to go to church in town.

The town is Petaluma, and the church is St. Vincent's Catholic Church, which is the church of Mary Lou's family and where we were married thirty-nine years before. This is the quietest day I have ever seen in this former farm town. The church has a few people in it already. We sit and say a prayer for the victims of 9/11.

It will take a couple of days to find out the details of this most awful day in New York. We know we will try to get back to New York as soon as possible. It will take a couple of days to settle things on the ranch, which hardly matters because all flights in and out have been canceled anyway.

We know we will be going back to many funerals and memorials for those who will never be found.

That night, our son Brandt and his wife, Joelle, with their daughter, Annie, come up to keep us company. Brandt is a dairyman who computerizes large dairy herds in the Central Valley. It is good to have them near us. Mary Lou's sister June and her husband Manuel also come down from Sacramento to be with us. This is all distracting and comforting.

Our daughter, Erika, a Cardiac Care Unit nurse, calls from time to time. She is a great comfort to us also. She is eight months pregnant with her first child, who will turn out to be a beautiful baby girl named Britta. This beautiful event, coming three weeks after all this sadness, is like sunshine through the storm.

Every so often, Leif calls from his fire company, Ladder 102, in Brooklyn's Bedford-Stuyvesant section. Theirs is the only firehouse in that battalion where the men working that day had not all been killed. Responding to the World Trade Center emergency, Ladder 102 had been dispatched to the Brooklyn Battery Tunnel below because it was thought people were trapped down there. That simple redirection saved all their lives that day.

Pretty early on, Leif has the tentative list of fire department personnel who have perished at the World Trade Center. It is worse than I could have ever imagined. Though it is painful for both of us, Leif reads the list to me. There is at least one person on that list who does not belong there. As he reads the names and companies they were in, he also often knows the names of those I know. Many are very good friends, one of my best friends, and there are many others that I went to fires with, ate with, and lived with. They are of all ranks. As he goes though the list, at each recognized name, the wind comes out of me. He asks me if I'm okay. I tell him to continue, I want to hear each name, as painful as it is.

It will take 40 minutes to read the list of names and their companies to me. When he's finished, there will be a hundred that were a part of my life and at least sixteen more who are the sons of friends of mine. There are brothers, fathers, and sons.

Joe Angelini, a good friend I worked with in Rescue 1 for many years, died there, along with his son, Joe Jr., of Ladder Company 4.

John Vigiano, a very respected and decorated captain who I knew for many years, lost both of his sons there; John was a firefighter in Ladder Company 132; his brother Joseph was with Police Emergency 2.

The one person on that list who did not belong there was one of the few survivors. There weren't many. It was my good friend and study mate, Captain Al Fuentes. He was buried in debris with head injuries and partially scalped; having aspirated a terrible amount of World Trade Center particulate matter into his lungs, he was possibly twenty minutes from death when he was found by rescuers. His harrowing, heroic fight for life and the effect of this experience on his family, especially his wife Eileen, the ordeal of locating where he was hospitalized and his subsequent battle for survival is detailed in his book, "American By Choice." I couldn't read this book without tears in my eyes.

Bill Bessman, John McAllister, Barry Meade, and I all studied with Al for a couple of years, for our test for promotion to lieutenant. Though Al was the youngest, he was the spark plug for our study group and the most knowledgeable in the ways of the test we would face. The amount of material to cover and organize to study for promotion is awesome. The commitment to the group is like a marriage of sorts. You can either get to hate each other and divorce or stay married and get to appreciate and respect each other. We all stayed together and we all made it. Three of us had over twenty years in the fire department and Al had a lot to do with it. This big, tough, open bear of a man and his return to life from the list of the dead was a true bright spot where there were not many—Al, the man who would kiss me and make me hug and kiss him whenever we met.

A week later, we get a flight back to New York. This isn't just any ordinary trip back and our country has just suffered the worst attack in its history. I want to display my defiance and pride in being an American, so I wear a western shirt of stars and stripes. At Oakland Airport, when we get up to the ticket counter, the airline representative, a very pleasant-looking older man is smiling broadly at me. He says, "You made my day!" His reaction makes my day.

CHAPTER 3

The World Trade Center Site—Ground Zero

It's late afternoon of what will be a rainy shift down at the World Trade Center site. Leif and I meet the city bus that's been assigned to take each shift of firefighters from Queens down to the lower Manhattan devastation. It's a convoy of about 15 buses, each filled with the gloomy night's shift.

All the men are in their firefighting gear. I'm in my own personal gear and since I retired just six years before, I fit in. Lieutenant Phil Chiaravino, the officer of Ladder 102 has given me permission to accompany Leif and this very experienced crew, to work at the site, doing what they've been doing for the last eight days, searching voids in the debris, digging and tunneling—with all that entails.

The convoy of buses stops a couple of city blocks north of the World Trade Center. We disembark onto West Street, which is covered with dust and a slurry of World Trade Center debris. It looks like a road in a third world country.

It's a dismal, wet night as I get off the bus and bump into two men with whom I had worked in Rescue 1. They are both captains now. These are men I know well, and had many experiences with. One is Mike Fitzgerald, who was also my son George's lieutenant in 44 Truck, and the other is John Carroll, a former college football player. We are all good friends and glad to see each other. I attempt to shake hands with John and he says, "Don't you shake hands with me, you F——." He embraces me in a bear hug. I have to run to make sure I don't lose the crew of 102 Truck in this sea of thousands of firefighters streaming down West Street, descending on Ground Zero.

Before we are at the site, I can hear the noise of portable generators. There is the sound of cranes and other heavy equipment being used to help ironworkers, who are cutting twisted steel beams for removal to allow deeper exploration of thousands of voids made by this pile that had been the World Trade Center. As we get nearer, I can see huge, low flatbed trucks that have already been loaded with maybe only one enormous twisted steel beam, working their way out of the pit.

As we are working our way around the site, I am trying to take in the incomprehensible devastation, the likes of which I have never seen in my life. All my years in the fire department, with all the collapses and all the other destruction to buildings I've seen over many years, have not prepared me for this.

I'm looking at the flood-lit, jagged, splintered remains of the metal facade, sticking out above fifty-foot piles of what is left of the thirteen-hundred-foot towers. Eight days after the attack of 9/11, smoke is everywhere, especially coming up out of the many voids in the piles of debris. The smoke swirls up around the eerily lit shards of the facade, which resembles the bombed-out ruins of a cathedral. Even in the rain, there is still dust in the air. Thousands of protected spots are still covered with dust. We are walking in wet slurry that is the same gray color as the dust. It is half a foot thick in many places. I know that this slurry we are walking in is the result of the compression and heat of these buildings coming down.

Thousands upon thousands of phones, computers, consoles of every kind, desks, chairs, partitions, and human beings, atomized together by this catastrophic collapse, combined with the rain, make up this gray slurry and dust. Amazingly, there are no large pieces of anything other than the steel beams themselves. Most everything was totally pulverized and obliterated.

This is Leif's eighth day at Ground Zero. We are now about at what was the south side of the Plaza and South Tower, by Liberty Street; there is that lingering glimmer of hope of finding someone alive, but all I can see is danger and death.

After trying to take this all in, my first words to Leif are: "Don't get hurt here." I am totally overwhelmed by the magnitude of this whole operation. If there is anybody alive—not likely—how could you get to them? There are literally thousands of voids and places where they could be and the removal of the massive, twisted steel blocking any chance of rescue or recovery is daunting, to say the least. The ironworkers and other construction crews will be doing this for months to come. God bless these guys.

What's amazing is that as we walk into this site with a couple of thousand other firefighters, this 16-acre site just devours them. There are so many operations going on simultaneously that there are groups of firefighters everywhere on the site on this dreary night.

Ladder 102, as are many others, is moving what they can to expose more voids. This is going on all over the site. There are many bucket brigades for daisy chains to remove particulate debris from the site. This goes on continuously.

At one point in the evening, a pair of FBI agents come up to me, a man and a woman. Probably because they can tell by my helmet that I'm an officer, they hand me an object and ask: "What do you think this is?" I examine it. It's flattened, very dirty, and blackened, but it's the shape and size of a fire helmet frontpiece; of course, this is where my mind is. I tell them that. The woman FBI agent says to me: "We think it is bone." I still have it in my hand and look closer and now I know what it is, and I say, "You're right, it is a human scapula." I have the remains, the shoulder blade, of one of the victims in my hand. This is very moving considering this person was alive eight days ago. I am sure this type of thing will happen thousands of times over the coming months and the body parts will be put into recovery buckets for future examination. So little that remains of living, breathing, loving, feeling human beings. Someone's son or daughter, father or mother, husband or wife.

During the night when things slow down, as they do, I walk around to Church Street to observe the many other operations going on at the same time. I am trying to get every perspective I can. I feel I owe this to my many friends who have died here, two-thirds of whom will never be recovered. It is impossible to take in this amount of destruction, but I try.

I hear somebody has found a hand and it gets everyone's attention. There is a fire officer at the bottom of a series of ladders that traverse the jagged twisted steel down into a void below grade. He's calling for something to put the hand into.

As I walk around or through the site I run into firefighters and officers I've known over the years. Many are standing by, in the shadows, in brown Carhart bib overalls with their fire helmets identifying them. As the cranes move steel, new openings are formed and these crews paw their way through them, looking for anything they can find of their brother firefighters and civilian victims. This is somber business. There is always some banter between firefighters, but here there is none. Even the living are wounded.

I pass restaurants that have been damaged to different degrees. All are full of dust, but cleaned enough to cook and feed the rescue and recovery workers. Many were fine restaurants that now have taken on the appearance of soup kitchens or food factories. Some will do this for months. Some will survive and some will not. But it is heartening and humbling to see this outpouring from people giving everything they have for nothing in return.

There are big day cruise boats and yachts tied up at North River's edge. They are serving wonderful meals in their comfortable dining rooms and the people organizing this are gracious to all who come there for an escape to something like normalcy. There are even women offering massages to anyone eating there. After eating, there are some who take them up on it. All the work down at Ground Zero is backbreaking, dirty work.

The rain has not let up the whole night. It's about midnight and it's time to leave the site and walk back to the buses. Everyone is damp and dirty. We run into Steve Geraghty, a captain who's down here, like many others, looking for his brother, Eddie, a battalion chief in the Ninth Battalion. He is missing and feared dead. I worked in Rescue 1 with Eddie years ago and knew him very well. He was a friend. It appears that Steve is not leaving as we say goodnight to him.

The whole area is barricaded off with National Guard troops. As we pass north to where the buses are, there are civilians carrying large thermoses with different kinds of drinks, including coffee. They run from person to person, offering what they have.

We get on the buses and the convoy goes north along West Street. Everyone's dulled, dirty, wet, and tired. It is raining very hard and the crowds that lined West Street earlier with all their signs of encouragement and love have dwindled some. But all along the way, there still are people, old and young, standing in this downpour of rain at twelve o'clock, in the dark, with signs that say, "FDNY, we love you." "You are in our hearts." "God bless America and the FDNY." Etc., etc. It brings tears to my eyes, seeing these people doing whatever they can to render their hearts to us. This, on a miserable, gloomy, dark New York City's West Street, at midnight.

CHAPTER 4

Leif's First Sight of Ground Zero

On the morning of September 11, 2001, the traffic going into the city was so heavy, Leif often had to drive on the shoulder of the road on his 50-mile trip to report into the Brooklyn firehouse, Ladder 102.

When he got there, the battalion had a bus that would bring all the recalled firefighters to the World Trade Center. Many of the firefighters were from fire companies where all the men who had been working that day were dead and many were never to be recovered. Living, breathing people—full of life before—who had ceased to exist.

Like veterans who have been in combat, Leif doesn't talk about that day very much. It has taken a long time to get details of what it was like two hours after the attack on America at the World Trade Center, Ground Zero.

Before heading out to Manhattan, the recalled firefighters were assigned into groups of five firefighters and an officer.

Upon getting to lower Manhattan, on roadways cleared for personnel responding in, they were struck by the mushroom cloud of smoke and debris—millions upon millions of pieces of paper, flying around—as Leif said, "Shit everywhere."

There were staging areas for groups of firefighters reporting in. But due to the fact that many chiefs, including Chief of Department Pete Ganci, were killed, the daunting attempt at organization did not take place right away. With no blame to anyone, the early stages of rescue and recovery would be taken on by small groups of officers and firefighters breaking off from the cluster that was the early effort at organizing a deeply wounded, traumatized FDNY. Like the early stages of battle in war, they are won by small batches of people doing what they have to, without high-up leadership, until stability and cohesion can be reestablished.

Leif's small group moved off into Ground Zero, 16 acres of the former World Trade Center, Plaza and Complex with its utter devastation. They came upon some members of Engine 209, the engine company housed with Ladder 102. Of course, they are in psychological shock. Their survival is due only to the fact they were able to run for their lives when the South Tower came down. At this time, all the firefighters from all the fire companies that came from their area in Brooklyn, except Ladder 102 and Engine 209, are dead, other than a couple of motor pump operators (engineer chauffeurs), who survived due to the fact that they traditionally stay with the pumper apparatus. One of the men from Engine 209 has blood coming from his eyes and ears, appearing like a stigmata in this devil-made hell.

Leif couldn't be sure whether he heard Vibra-Alert alarms from fallen firefighters or not. The Vibra-Alert alarm is turned on at every operation and worn by every firefighter. If something happens and a firefighter is rendered unconscious or incapacitated, the loud, piercing, chirping alarm will help locate him. Initially, these chirping alarms were going off all over the 16 acres, which was often described as sounding like a field of crickets. These were all from fallen firefighters—hundreds of them, all at once. On top of this, every other conceivable alarm—car alarms, smoke alarms, fire alarms, and alarms of every other electronic or mechanical device—was going off at the same time, all day long. Bedlam.

These first hours and the rest of this awful day will be filled with sheer danger: falling debris from existing structures; multiple massive fires; unbearably acrid black smoke from every material known to man; broken, crushed, and particulate debris of human beings. This was the Fire Department New York of September 11, 2001. There are many dead and missing, the firefighters working that day will never be the same again. That is why some say that there are three FDNYs: the Pre-9/11 FDNY, the FDNY of 9/11, and the Post-9/11 FDNY.

Leif, like his older brothers, had opportunities to spend nights with Rescue 1 and to respond with them. For more than 16 of their growing-up years, I was in Rescue 1 and they had a lot of exposure to it through being there themselves or through my tales of exciting things with which the rescue company got involved. Like all firefighters' kids, the fire company their father was in became a part of their own lives. It became part of the bedrock of their upbringing.

Leif would later tell me that when he saw Rescue 1's tandem-axled truck, with its ass-end sticking up in the air out of the rubble that had been the World Trade Center, it was a defining moment for him. Sadly, it was also an indicator of how deeply this attack shook our foundations.

CHAPTER 5

Kathy's Letter

This letter is from our 12-year-old niece from Aurora, Colorado. Her letter and my response clarify many things about the fire department, as well as showing how firefighters desire to pass on their knowledge and stories to keep others safe.

February 23, 1989

Dear Uncle George,

How are you?

My reading class has to do reports on different kinds of topics. My friends, Tom and Chris, picked firefighting. They have a few questions. How do you fight different fires? What rules do you have to follow in case of a fire? What kind of equipment do pumper trucks, ladder trucks and rescue trucks have? How do smoke detectors work? I was also wondering if they could use the video cassette that you sent us out once before. If you can't, it's ok. Please write back soon.

Love, Kathy
P.S. Thank you.

March 6, 1989

Dear Kathy,

Thank you for your letter and I'll try as best as I can to answer your questions.

I've been a fireman for 24 years in the City of New York. The last 15 years, I've worked as a member of Rescue Company 1, the only company of its kind in Manhattan, and the first company of its kind in the United States. Previous to this, I worked in Ladder Company 102 for five years and Engine Company 230 for five years, both in Brooklyn.

An engine company is the company that carries the hose and its members put out the fire. The ladder company carries portable ladders of various lengths and one 75- to 100-foot hydraulic aerial ladder. The rescue company in New York has a large Mack truck van that carries special heavy tools for unusual fires, emergencies, and collapses.

The three things that make a fire are: 1–fuel (house & personal belongings), 2–heat, and 3–oxygen supply (as from the air). To fight a fire, we have to deprive the fire of either its fuel or its heat or its oxygen supply. There are several ways we can do this.

We can rob the fire of fuel by covering the burning material with foam or chemical powder, but this is very expensive to do. We can deprive the fire of oxygen also by application of foam and certain other chemicals, which is also very expensive. Although doing these things is very effective on fire, in most cases, besides being expensive, there is not a ready supply of them. But we do have one more thing that is not expensive and that we have a lot of. That is water. Water primarily cools the fire by robbing it of heat. When a lot of water is used, it may also smother the fire, robbing it of oxygen. Water cools best when used as a fog and smothers best when used as a solid stream.

Enginemen, the men with the pumper, take their hose and hook it up to the pumper and crawl to the seat of the fire in the building to put the fire out. Often, lives are saved by the enginemen putting the fire out.

The laddermen ventilate the building by cutting a hole in the roof and opening or breaking windows opposite the way the enginemen will be coming with the hose. At the same time, laddermen are searching the building for unconscious or trapped victims.

There are times that firemen putting out fires become trapped themselves and someone must save them. In New York City, they formed the rescue company to do just that. Because the rescue carries special tools like the Hurst Tool Jaws of Life, various jacks, saws, cutting torches, and many other emergency-type tools, the rescue company is sometimes used for non-fire emergencies, like auto accidents and building collapses. The rescue company also has scuba-diving equipment and qualified divers for water emergencies, such as cars that go off piers or downed airplanes.

Years ago, when most things were made out of natural materials, the smoke from the fire was not as dangerous to a fireman. Today, many things in the home are made out of chemicals that, when burning, give off poisonous gases that are extremely injurious to firemen as well as civilians. That is why today when you see firemen, they almost always are wearing self-contained breathing apparatus (air supply masks). Many more victims die from smoke rather than fire. That is why smoke detectors are so important in saving lives.

Smoke detectors work in one of two ways. Those that detect the chemical reaction of smoke before it can even be seen by the human eye are called ionization detectors and they are the best ones. There is another kind of fire detector that detects the density of the smoke by the degree of light. This stage of detection is later than ionization.

Before fire breaks out, the material often smolders for a long time and it is at this time that many victims die of suffocation from the poisonous gases given off. At the very first sign of smoke, the smoke detector alarm goes off, alerting people before the smoke has a chance to build up to dangerous levels.

Every home should have at least one smoke detector on every level because they will warn you before smoke can build up or break into fire and kill you and your family.

If you have a fire in your house, it is important to alert everybody in your house that you can, closing all doors behind you, and getting out as soon as possible. Immediately call the fire department and have a meeting place outside of your house where everyone knows to go to be sure everyone is out of the house. Do not for any reason go back into a house that is on fire. If there is anyone unaccounted for from your family, notify the first fireman on the scene of this fact and the possible location of this person. Once you are out, **NEVER GO BACK IN!!!**

I hope I have answered all of your questions and that this will be helpful to your friends, Tom and Chris.

Love,
Uncle George

CHAPTER 6

The Ladies on the Roof

One can't walk, and the other can't see. There they are, standing huddled and holding each other, with no place to go. Kind of looking like they are waiting for a bus. The only thing is, they aren't waiting for a bus; they are on the roof of an eight-story building with the building burning beneath them.

About 11:00 a.m. on December 9, 1976, a working fire is reported by alarm to Rescue 1, at Forty-Third Street, between Tenth and Eleventh avenues. We are housed in the 1894 brick firehouse that had been the quarters of the disbanded Engine Company 2. The signal coming in is for a 10-75, an all-hands working fire, at an alarm box near Second Avenue and East Sixth Street. That's clear across Manhattan, but rescue responds to all working fires below 125th Street, so we respond to that location.

On our way there, a second alarm is sent for this box. This is a major fire now and we know we will be going to work.

When we get there, an aerial ladder is raised to the corner of the roof of the eight-story building. There is fire coming out some of the top floor windows on the Second Avenue side and some from the East Sixth Street side. The windows on the corner under the aerial do not have fire out of them yet. Captain Bill Anderson, a former Marine, orders us to the roof via the aerial ladder on the corner. It is extended just about maximally at a very steep angle.

We climb the ladder to the roof with all of our tools, including a power saw, which we intend to use to open the roof. It's a long climb, giving us time to see that this is going to be a tough job.

Rescue is going to the roof because, in most cases, they are sent above the fire, because it is the most exposed area for fire extension and people being trapped.

As we mount the roof, I see these two old women standing on the Sixth Street side, bundled in their winter coats, scarves on their heads, holding their handbags and each other. They are a pathetic sight.

I can't imagine how they got to the roof. The stairway to the roof bulkhead at the back is already spewing ugly black and brown marshmallow smoke out its door.

Firefighters from the ladder companies are everywhere on the roof, sizing things up and opening up what they can. This is a big roof with eight stories below it.

I make eye contact with these two old women and I assure them that we will not go anywhere without them. We won't forget them.

As bad as things look on a roof, at times, we hardly ever sense the danger we feel when attacking the fire inside. I know they are there and for the time being, I think they are safe. So I join the team of other firefighters on the roof, opening up.

As we cut holes to vent the cockloft, between the top floor and the roof, there is tremendous heat and smoke coming out of every opening. The top floor, 100 feet by 100 feet, is fully involved in fire. The fire is now a three-alarm fire and there are no adjacent buildings of the same height to step onto. This is one of those times it is truly dangerous to be on the roof. For all intents and purposes, we have an isolated building, with the whole top floor untenable.

What had been a clear and sunny day has turned into something else on this roof. I look at the women and the smoke that is billowing around them with each gust of the cold, 30-mph wind. It has taken on an ominous blackness that has turned the roof to night. It is suddenly awful.

What has happened is that fire has completely come out of all 10 windows on the Second Avenue side and all 10 windows on the Sixth Street side. Blown by high winds, the fire from the street-side, top-floor windows has leaped onto the roof.

There is always some jeopardy on any roof of a fire building, especially when the top floor is involved, but it is relatively rare that it will come to a "run for your life" situation. This is one of those times.

The lapping of the fire onto the roof is so sudden that we firefighters have to find our own way off from wherever we are. A couple of them make it to the aerial ladder before it is taken away from the building so it will not be exposed to the fire.

As Captain Bill Anderson disappears into the smoke, looking for a way off, he yells, "Somebody get the women."

When it comes time to get the women, they are already on my mind, as I had made eye contact and extended assurances to them earlier.

The younger of the two women, the one who can't see, is whisked off by a young truckman from Ladder Company 3. They disappear deeper into the smoke.

I find myself alone with the older woman, who appears to be about 80 years old. She can't walk, so I kind of drag her on her feet, to the only way I know, the rear. There is no fire escape on our side of the rear of the building. This is the only way I can think of that we can get away.

Out of desperation, I get her to the bulkhead above the interior stairs. It is about 15 feet from the rear. With the smoke and heat coming out from below, I know it will be almost impossible for me alone to get down there, and I am saddled with this old lady I cannot leave behind.

Interestingly, years later at the World Trade Center on September 11, 2001, I believe this situation prevailed in many places where firefighters were committed to people who needed their help and they could not leave them. Firefighters died that day because they would not run when others couldn't.

Just as I get near the bulkhead door with the nasty heat and smoke there, Bill Riley comes out of nowhere. He sees that I've got this woman by the shoulders and I know he is thinking the same thing I am: "This is our only way out." He says, "Let me go down and see if we can get past the top floor." He is gone about 10 to 15 seconds. I'm thinking, how did he ever get down to the top floor, it is so hot and the smoke couldn't be denser. He comes back and says, "There is no way we can get down that way."

At this time, we hear the captain calling from across the bulkhead. Riley immediately heads that way and disappears through the dense terrible smoke and heat.

Now I'm alone with this old woman, who seems to be completely unaware of our situation. Bill Anderson sounds like he is calling through a tunnel: "George, you have got to get her through here, there is a door on this side." With all the smoke coming out of the bulkhead, it seems impossible that I can get through to the other side of the roof.

In desperation, I grab the lady's collar and drag her unceremoniously through to the other side, her legs dragging behind her. We make it through to what I think is a better situation, but it is actually not much better.

On the other side are the captains of Rescue 1 and Ladder 3, Bill Riley, and an old friend, Richie Jacquin, and other members of Ladder 3. They are all at the rear parapet, ready to mount the gooseneck ladder down to the fire escape on that side of the rear. On the top floor landing, the young truckman from Ladder 3 is guiding the ambulatory lady to the landing below the top floor. It is just a matter of time before fire breaks out of these rear windows.

My getting this woman to the gooseneck is causing further delay while the fire is now burning on the roof clear back to the bulkhead.

About four-fifths of the roof is on fire and if fire comes out those rear windows, we will all be finished.

Meanwhile, the young truckman is getting his charge down to the floor below the fire floor. I jump onto the gooseneck ladder and Bill Riley puts the old woman on the ladder inside my arms, so I can guide her down. She cannot move. I suggest putting her over my shoulder in a fireman's carry. Riley says to me, two octaves lower than he normally talks, "Oh no, George, she will be looking down eight stories." She says, "I weigh 160 pounds." She is about five feet tall, so she is shaped like a football. Over my shoulder is not a good idea. There are many anxious firefighters at that rear parapet, including a battalion chief.

I tell Riley to hold her collar and I'll pull her legs out and have her slide down to the top floor landing. Big, tough Bill Riley, always a gentleman, says, "Mom, let me hold your handbag." She snatches it toward herself, indicating that she has no idea the danger we are all in.

While Riley holds her collar and I pull her legs out, we guide her to the top floor fire escape landing. I look up and see all the others waiting at the parapet. Some one yells, "Get her down to the next floor." We do the same thing again and on the landing below the fire, I kick the stiles out of the window sashes in order to get the old woman inside to other firefighters who will bring her down through the interior. This opens the bottleneck that has kept the firefighters above in imminent danger.

Shortly after this, most of the roof collapses onto the top floor. The old lady gets her picture in the centerfold of the *Daily News*. She is being carried by two firefighters who, like her, have no idea where she came from and the mortal danger we had all been in.

CHAPTER 7

Waldbaum's Supermarket— August 2, 1978

At 9:02 on the morning of August 2, 1978, a second alarm has been transmitted for Brooklyn Box 3300 to all firehouses throughout the city. Everyone now knows that there is a working fire that could not be handled by the original assignment of three engines and two trucks. Another full assignment is needed, signaling the fire is not under control and there's danger of further exposure to other property or people.

At Rescue 1 this morning, we are just starting our day. Bobby Burns and I are sitting in the kitchen at the back of the apparatus floor, formerly the stable for the horses in the late nineteenth and early twentieth centuries. We're enjoying one more cup of coffee before we get on with maintenance of the many tools of this heavy rescue company and the things that are done every day to keep order in the house.

We have more than casual interest in the fire in Brooklyn. We know that Rescue 2, the Brooklyn rescue company, is there already or on their way. More than likely they were rolling on the 10-75, the signal for a working fire.

It isn't often that Rescue 1 is called to back up the rescue units in the other boroughs, mainly because Manhattan has such high population density and so many large and unusual buildings. For that matter, it's not routine to take any rescue company out of its respective borough.

Things can change very fast at any time in the fire service. Between 9:17 and 9:18, a third alarm and a fourth alarm are transmitted for Box 3300, Brooklyn. This is a dire signal to us.

Bobby Burns and I are very experienced hands at this time and we know that back-to-back multiple alarms transmitted from the same location are harbingers of firemen in trouble.

Bobby goes right away to the bitch box in the kitchen that reaches anywhere in the house. "Moose, get ready to go to Brooklyn." Moose is Bill Curran, the chauffeur of the rescue today. He no sooner gets it out of his mouth when the Manhattan dispatcher comes on: "Rescue 1, respond to Brooklyn Box 44-3300."

All fire or emergency alarms are taken with utmost seriousness, but the gravity of the rescuers being in trouble raises the alarm to a whole new level. We could be them.

This type of call is the reason for the rescue company's existence in the first place. Back in 1915, the Chief of Department, John J. Kenlon, formed Rescue 1, an idea that came from the Germans. The main reason was that there were terrible fires south of Houston Street in lower Manhattan. It wasn't called "Hell's Hundred Acres" for no reason. The enormous loft buildings were heavily loaded with plumbing supplies and heavy machinery and they were prone to collapse under heavy fire conditions. Many firemen were trapped and killed down there. A special company of big men who could make use of the 75-pound Draeger Rebreathing Mask to aid in the rescue of those trapped was formed. Rescue 1 was the first heavy rescue company of its kind in the United States.

We are out the door and on our way, responding to Brooklyn. Responding in the traffic in Manhattan through the Brooklyn-Battery Tunnel to Brooklyn takes time. On the way, we hear that there has been a collapse with firemen missing.

A little before 10:00, we arrive near Ocean Avenue and Avenue Y, the site of the fourth alarm, Box 44-3300, Brooklyn.

As we get off the rig, a lieutenant comes behind the rig and tells us, "Ten guys are missing." It is so surreal I can hardly believe what I am hearing. It is hard to absorb that number, considering the impact of the death of one fireman, never mind ten men missing.

Lieutenant Jimmy Curran leads us down Avenue Y to the building on fire. It's a Waldbaum's Supermarket on the corner of Ocean Avenue and Avenue Y. As we approach, my very first thought is that I'm looking at an erupting cauldron. Fire and heavy smoke are belching out from over the one-story, 20-foot-high brick wall. A large part of the roof is gone and the fire, smoke, and heat are vented to the open sky; it looks awful.

My very next thought is, "Where can the missing men be?" We get to a small door along Avenue Y, about 20 feet from what appears to be the rear of the building. There's a one-and-three-quarter-inch hoseline disappearing into it. Jimmy Curran, a smart and very aggressive officer, has already gotten our orders.

He says to me, "George, we're going to relieve Rescue 2 on this line." I say, "Jimmy, let's not get tied down to a hoseline here."

I should have known better. Jimmy says, "It's not what you think, we're going to use the line for protection to move further into the building where the missing men may be." We are right at the door entrance when two of the remaining members of Rescue 2 come out, following the hoseline, crawling over the debris inside the door. These are two very decorated, tough guys. They are whipped. Their faces are the color of tomatoes, pouring sweat, long strands of mucous hanging from their noses. They look like their heads could pop. They are wearing their Scott Air Paks on their backs with the face pieces hanging down, as are ours.

These two are Jack Klehaas and Pete Bondy. Jack had been in 108 Truck at the same time I was in 102 Truck and would eventually become a chief.

By the looks of them, they don't have to tell us how bad it is in there. Jimmy leads the way with me following right behind him, Mike Walsh is behind me, and Mike is followed by Bobby Burns. Crawling over the debris, not too far in, we get to the nozzle for the hoseline. I'm relieved that Jimmy tells me to take it as we crawl in. To make any headway in here, we will need water for our protection. Now, I'm very glad I've got the nozzle with the water. A former engineman never fails to appreciate water.

As bad as it looks outside, nothing can prepare me for what is inside. The massive, timbered, bolted trusses, which had spanned 100 feet, are broken and collapsed from fire. Large sections of roof sheathing, still tied together, are draped over the broken trusses. There is fire and smoke everywhere, coming out from underneath the plywood sheathing. The heat comes in waves and it rocks us. There is a lot of fire all around and underneath us, lapping out from under what had been the roof. At any time, fire could break out under us and we would be cooked. The smoke is terrible.

We can't put our face pieces on because it would cut down on our situational awareness, which is critical when there is so much fire underneath us. On the other hand, the environment is so dangerous we can't take a chance on going in without them. From the start, I would've liked the comfort of the mask. However, there is no way to put it on and negotiate over the remains of the broken trusses and roofing while looking for missing men.

When we went through the door, I truly didn't think we could last in there for five minutes. Although the sky is open above us and at times we can see some of the beautiful summer morning sky, it is terrible down here in this cauldron. Brother firemen are missing and I'm thinking, "I don't want some half-hearted so-and-so coming to get me." I'm sure thoughts like these keep us all going.

There are one or two large-caliber streams being played over the ten thousand square feet of fire destruction from a tower ladder. As we move further in over the top, there are times we are on the broken truss beams. The one-and-three-quarters-inch hoseline seems really inadequate. Jimmy keeps us moving. When he's working, he is Lieutenant Curran, but all of us working today have 12 or more years in the job and we all worked in the rescue company with him as a fireman. It's just us in this awful place, so he's "Jimmy." I tell him, "Jimmy, this isn't enough water." He says, "I'll call for a backup line."

We are moving toward the center of the rear of the store. We are unaware that most of the other activity going on is in the front of the store on Ocean Avenue. Firefighters are trying to get deeper in where there are still ceilings suspended on top of the aisles of shelving. They know that some of the men who escaped were on the roof when it collapsed, and fell through the ceiling to the floor.

About this time, Pete Bondy shows up in back of us. I thought that when he got out, that would be it for him. Well, the fact is, these kind of men never give up. My guess is he and Jack got around to the front, saw what was going on and he came back to work toward the front from the rear.

We are crawling on the trusses and sheathing, and as eddies of smoke lift, we sometimes can see openings and ceiling parts. A couple of aisle spaces are open below us and both Pete Bondy and Bobby Burns climb down into them. All of a sudden, one of them calls out, "We've found a six-foot hook." The two of them bound over the shelf to the next aisle, where they are below us. We are above them with the hoseline on the broken truss. "We've got a helmet." It's a truckman's helmet, identified by a red frontpiece. We all know we are close.

Within seconds of finding the helmet, Jimmy is now standing, looking down. He is right in back of me, kind of looking down and a little back to the area we've just passed over, toward the aisle that Pete and Bobby are pawing in. Jimmy yells, "There they are." I'm standing right next to Jimmy and I'm looking at the same spot. At first, I can't see anything. The smoke lifts and lightens a little and I see what Jimmy has seen moments before. Like two apparitions in the smoky haze, lying spread-eagled, supine, totally intact with all their fire clothing, minus helmets, are two of the firefighters. They are lying on top of the ceiling tin that's draped over shelves above and next to where Bobby and Pete are—a ghostly and unreal sight.

The fact that they are on their backs, spread out like they are, makes me think, "Death came fast." A blessing.

Those who got out from between the ceiling and roof onto the floor were lucky enough to fall further toward the front, where super-heated air and fire did not kill them instantly, enabling them to scramble out. A couple of these men are burned pretty bad, but they will make it.

Alerted by the sight of the two dead firefighters, I scan around instinctively. I look down into the space right next to and slightly further in from them. It's very smoky down there and I'm looking at roofing materials, tar, and rolls of tar paper. Then I see the entrails of a human being. I immediately leave the line to Mike Walsh and jump down into the pit.

I know for sure that there is one person down here. There is a mess of tar over everything. Roof work has been going on before this fire. Then I start pulling at things to expose something identifiable. Just like that, I realize that there are at least three men down in this tarred mess.

Jimmy, standing above, asks me, "How many are there?" I tell him, "I think three." "How do you know?" he asks. I tell him, "I can feel the bodies of three men underneath me." He says, "Not good enough, count heads." I confirm that there are three bodies and I am sure I have three heads. "Jimmy, I think there's a fourth. I think I have his shoulder." Now I feel down in this blackened, ashy tar to see if I can reach a head attached to the shoulder, only to discover I already have the head of the fourth man. His head is so hyper-extended that his chin, sticking out of the tar, resembles a shoulder. All four are on their backs. When the collapse into the fire occurred, others who were there said they heard screams. Any screaming came from those who lived. These six men died instantly.

Other men are now in this pit with me, trying to sort out the jumbled pile of bodies encased in tar and roofing material. Firemen on their way home from their night tours and some at home, hearing radio reports of men missing, are responding on their own and start to show up.

At first, I'm too busy to notice who's there. It's not a big space we're in. There's not a lot of room but, understandably, everyone wants to help. Jesse Bilboa, Dennis Horrigan, and Dick Martinsen have crawled in here also, having just gotten off the night tour. There are still four men unaccounted for, so other things are still happening like further searches and breaching the outside brick wall on Avenue Y, not far from the door where we came in.

This is terrible, hard work, untangling the bodies of our brother firemen from this mess. There is no even ground to stand on and as respectful as we are toward our dead brothers, we can't help but accidentally step or kneel on them in order to free them from each other and all of this tarred muck.

I'm becoming more aware of the other men around me now. There's Bobby Burns, Mike Walsh, Jesse Bilboa, and another man. I find out later he is Tommy McTigue of Rescue 3. We are all working with one another to get our fallen brothers out of here. We are at the same time looking for the other missing men, as are firefighters in other parts of the building. Everyone at this site has been spurred on by our finding these six men.

The conditions that were so awful when we first got in here are not even a consideration anymore. It is still hot and smoky and the large-caliber water streams are probably having a positive effect. For those of us in the hole, our whole focus is on the job at hand.

Battalion Chief Bill Cooper, a former Rescue 1 lieutenant, shows up above us. One of these fallen men is his driver. He tells us everyone's accounted for. The missing and dead are these six firemen we have found. It's a strange kind of relief, considering we have six confirmed dead that we have personally seen and are still working to free four of them.

Apparently, some of the men who fell through the roof but were fortunate enough to scramble or fall through the ceiling onto the store floor were rushed to hospitals before they could be accounted for. That was probably how the original number of 10 missing was reported.

Our work to free these four dead men continues, while more and more men keep showing up at the scene. Daisy chains of many firefighters and officers are needed to pass the bodies of their brothers to each other in order to get them over the smoking, hot, collapsing rubble and debris.

The breached hole through the brick wall that had been made while there was still hope the missing men would be reached and found alive is now being used to get the dead firemen to the outside. The two men found on top of the shelving and ceiling tin have been removed this way.

As we untangle the dead men, they are all whole, in their fire clothing. If I knew them personally, I would recognize them. As we lift them out, one by one, you notice little things. The officer is wearing his radio and his red and blue pens are still in his officer's shirt pocket. He looks just like he is asleep.

It takes about another hour and a half to complete the task of getting them all out. One by one, we put them in body bags and they are carried out of the pit and over the pile to the outside hole by a stream of somber, respectful brother firemen.

We would be inside that burning and collapsed supermarket for a couple of hours till the last fallen fireman was out. And I'd thought the conditions were so bad we couldn't last five minutes.

We are released from Box 44-3300 and, just like that, return to Manhattan. A lot of things were happening around us this day and we did our part. We are tired, but ready for the next alarm. We are back in service.

Amazingly, when we get to the old firehouse in Manhattan, we are reflective but have a quiet late lunch. At this time, there is no post-trauma therapy. We are each other's therapy.

CHAPTER 8

The Rescue Company

The idea for a heavy rescue company came from the Germans. They had special companies of sappers and miners attached to the fire service. These companies were there primarily to reach and rescue people trapped in collapsed buildings. There were no such companies in New York or, for that matter, in the rest of America.

In 1915, Chief of Department John J. Kenlon, FDNY, formed Rescue Company 1 in Manhattan, the first heavy rescue company in America.

Because New York City was a large city with many aging buildings and newer buildings getting bigger and more complex, the danger of collapse under fire conditions was becoming greater, not just for civilians, but for the firemen as well. When collapses occurred, the fire department was inadequately equipped and trained to handle them.

Lower Manhattan south of Houston Street was loaded with huge loft buildings of heavy mill construction, many with cast-iron columns. These buildings were so big they were as deep as a city block. They were loaded with heavy machinery and material such as steel and plumbing supplies. Under fire conditions, there was great danger of being lost or trapped or caught in a collapsed building. To firemen, this was "Hell's Hundred Acres."

Heavy rescue meant big, specially trained men using big, heavy tools in order to reach trapped civilians and other firemen under every imaginable condition. Men with building trades skills and rigging expertise were given special consideration for candidacy to the rescue company.

Originally, Rescue 1 had a 1914 Cadillac Touring Car converted to an open tool van by the fire department shops. The special tools they started out with were rope and life belts, jacks, block and tackle (mechanical advantage) equipment, cutting torches, the Lyle Life Gun and the 75-pound Draeger Rebreathing Helmet (mask). The Lyle Gun, Draeger mask, and rope would become the insignia of the FDNY Rescue Company.

Ten years later, Rescue 2 was formed in Brooklyn; eventually there were Rescue 3 for the Bronx, Rescue 4 for Queens, and Rescue 5 for Staten Island.

Over the years, the rescue rigs (apparatus) would become bigger and bigger due to the accumulation of and need for more and more equipment. Nothing came off the rig for a very long time but eventually much more was added, including electrical generators, lights, inhalator/resuscitators, medical supplies, and many more hydraulic jacks and shores. Later, they added the Tirfor grip hoist and special 60-foot hard steel cable, steel trench jacks, smoke ejectors, and various chemicals and dry powders for oil and metal fires respectively. Other innovations included Hurst's Jaws of Life tool for vehicle extrications, air bags used in place of jacks, scuba gear with dry suits and tanks (originally for under-pier fires and the inevitable water rescues), and high angle rescue ropes and hardware for mountaineering techniques for carrying out rescues that are beyond the reach of ladders. Chain hoists and shackles as well as "Z" irons placed on the edge of train platforms for jacking a passenger train away from the platform to free someone caught in the opening. Wooden block setups, used in conjunction with jacks and air bags, enable the rescue company to separate train cars from their wheel trucks or lift both the car and truck off the track, depending on where the trapped victim is. The rescue company also carries oak cribbing and wedges of every size to prevent the opening that is being made from closing again on the trapped victim—"to hold what you've got."

On top of all that is the usual complement of shovels of every size, pavement breakers, chain saws, circular power saws, along with regular truck hand tools, such as the 10-pound steel "Halligan" lockbreakers, six-foot hooks, axes, and mauls.

Just about every 8 to 10 years, the rescue companies would receive a newer, bigger, redesigned, distinctive truck, from the "Bull Dog" Macks of the 1920s to the big Mack diesels. At first, the engine was forward; later, the cab was over the engines and there were tandem rear axles in order to handle the increasingly heavy loads. More can be found out about these interesting apparatus in Paul Hashagen's book "Fire Rescue—The History of FDNY, Rescue Company 1." Paul was a decorated and dedicated member of Rescue 1 while I was there.

Until the Brooklyn Waldbaum's Supermarket fire and roof collapse on August 2, 1978, there had only been one other time that all four rescues of New York City worked at the same job. Staten Island did not have a rescue company at this time. That was the Holland Tunnel fire of May 13, 1949. Battalion Chief Beake, FDNY, died of deadly fumes and many other firemen and civilians were injured and overcome by the smoke.

On September 11, 2001, all five rescue companies, Rescue 1, Manhattan; Rescue 2, Brooklyn; Rescue 3, The Bronx; Rescue 4, Queens; Rescue 5, Staten Island would be at the World Trade Center and all the men working that day would be killed there.

CHAPTER 9

Fire at Macy's

At 4:08 p.m., an alarm comes in for Manhattan Box 714, Macy's Department Store on West Thirty-Fourth Street. Rescue 1 is assigned on this box, along with the rest of the first alarm assignment. They include Engine 1 and Ladder 24 from West Thirty-First Street, along with Engines 26 and 65, Ladder 21, and the 9th Battalion Chief.

This box comes in from time to time in the form of automatic alarms from surges in water pressure in Macy's extensive sprinkler system. Although no alarm is treated routinely, we are all used to responding to this box. In the past, it always turned out to be nothing. Recently though, there have been a few instances of deliberate arson attempts with small, timed ignition devices placed in clothing on sales racks.

It's Thursday, June 14, 1979, a pleasant day. Earlier, around 2:00 p.m., we had been down that way at the quarters of Engine 1 and Ladder 24, exchanging our empty air bottles for full ones. While exchanging the bottles, I noticed a really big young truckman from Ladder 24 watching and listening to what was going on with us. Probably he had just finished lunch and was just relaxing in the front of the apparatus floor. It would turn out that he was Fireman Walter Smith.

When we get to Macy's on Thirty-Fourth Street, we are directed to a doorway midway between Seventh Avenue and Broadway. Engine 1 and Ladder 24's apparatus are parked out front.

The security people of Macy's lead us into the store on the first floor. Lieutenant Tony Limberg of the Rescue realizes quickly that we are being misdirected and tells them we want the closest stairway, which turns out to be back where we came from. This causes us about a minute's delay.

Someone tells us that the first due Engine Company 1 and the first due Ladder Company 24 are on the fifth floor. So we trudge up the stairs.

As we turn from the fourth-floor landing toward the fifth, I see the engine's hoseline hooked up to the standpipe outlet. The line is charged and I can hear the nozzleman clearing the hoseline with its rush of air, before the water.

I look up to the fifth-floor landing and cannot believe my eyes. There is Captain Bradley of Engine 1 and a couple of his men going to their knees as the most awful-looking, black, acrid, marshmallow smoke is bubbling out the doorway from the fifth floor of the store.

This store is considered the largest department store in the world. Each floor between Seventh Avenue and Broadway is the size of a football field. The area the smoke is coming from is about half of that. The other half is separated from the rest of the floor area by a firewall and fire doors.

Tony says, "Where's the truck?" Captain Bradley answers, "In there somewhere." I'm thinking, "In where?"

Just as we get to the fifth floor landing, the smoke has banked down, right to the floor. I'm familiar with this floor because I'd been in the sporting goods section of this store not too long ago. I can't believe that so much smoke is pushing like this out of such a big area.

As bad as it is, just knowing that there are guys in there makes us feel a need to find out where they are. Tony and I start to crawl through the double doors toward the fire area. We can't see a thing and I'm thinking, "Where the hell are they? How can they be functioning effectively in here?"

We're not through the doorway yet when, out of nowhere, we hear the terrible commotion of frantic men, running for their lives. All of a sudden, they are in the doorway with us. I get thrown to the side against the open door and they are scrambling out over Lieutenant Limberg's back, flattening him.

This has all taken place in one or two seconds. As we back out onto the landing, there is tremendous excitement and confusion. The officer and men of Ladder 24 are trying to catch their breath from the run for their lives. Without even catching his breath, the young, scarlet-faced, profusely perspiring lieutenant says loudly, "One of my men is still in there." I'm still thinking, "Where?" Tony and I gather ourselves to try to get in there again. We don't get 10 feet inside the door when we are hit with the unbearable heat that is now combined with the awful smoke. We are forced to back out, back onto the landing. There are a lot of men including Bill Riley and Norman Newkirk, both senior, experienced rescue men who had come to the Rescue from 26 Truck in Harlem. Steve Casani is there. We're considering how to get a large-caliber stream into the doorway. There is a lot of confusion. Each man has an idea as to what to do next. One of us is still in there and we are going to have to get him. This is a personal challenge for every fireman here.

In the middle of this turmoil, someone from down below says, "Everyone is accounted for." There are at least three companies of men on this landing, maybe 15 men or more. Each of us wants this to be so. We are more than ready to accept this.

The excitement is replaced by some relief, even though the fire conditions on the floor are worse than ever. The lieutenant of 24 Truck is looking down, shaking his head, and at the same time he utters, "I can't believe this is happening." I am standing right next to him. He grabs me by the arm and looks into my eyes and says, "Rescue, I'm telling you, my man is still in there." He has snapped me out of my momentary reverie. His desperate plea has personally entrusted and obligated me to the mission of finding and saving his lost man. It's the same for the other Rescue men there.

Things are happening very fast. To reemphasize our mission immediately, Norman says to me, with gravity, as only a former recon Marine can, "George, one of our men is still in there."

All of us are back to reality from our momentary false relief. Lieutenant Limberg is thinking of a large-caliber, multi-versal nozzle being put into the doorway in order to make headway. Norman Newkirk suggests breaching walls to get to the missing man. These are great ideas, but the area we are dealing with is half the size of a football field.

There is a hallway running along the Thirty-Fourth Street side, with offices on the outside and a wall on the inside. The inside wall is about 100 feet long. We can breach it, but where will that get us? We don't know where the missing man is and breaching that large fire area may cause further exposure problems. The wall is still providing protection from the enormous fire inside.

All of our attempts to get in the door are met with tremendous heat and the flood of water on the floor is burning our knees.

Other fire companies are making attempts to get into the fire area through the fire doors from the Broadway side of the building. Engine 65 is there and they are having their own problems.

Engine 1, backed by Engine 26, is having water pressure problems and that alone will rule out the use of a large-caliber stream. Too many sprinkler heads have fused open in there. They were dry due to the system being worked on, so now they are all open and taxing the water pumping capacities of the original engines at the scene.

Second, third, and fourth alarms have been transmitted, mainly to get water supplied to Macy's extensive standpipe hose system and the sprinkler system, which has hundreds of heads, all open on this advanced fire.

Eventually, there are many handlines being brought on to the fire by many engines from different and opposing positions. This in itself creates problems, with smoke and heat being driven by the engines toward each other.

The punishment on all the firemen there is unrelenting. We are always looking for the moment to get in there. There are ventilation problems due to partitioning along the outside of the fire and inside. These conditions are causing all of us to use our Scott Air Masks and we are using a lot of bottles.

As frustrating and exhausting as this is, we never give up trying to get in there. One of our guys is in there somewhere and we are all hoping he has found a safe refuge, but these terrible smoke and heat conditions have gone on for a couple of hours and it doesn't look good. In spite of all the water being put on this fire, we don't have it under control until it has consumed all the combustibles within the fireproof structure.

We are now able to get into the area, which is dark and hot with smoke from the smoldering, thoroughly burned debris throughout. It is a maze of the remains of racks that had been full of clothing and other stock. All the debris is within a foot of the floor, except for parts of racks, partitions, and wire.

It is very hard to distinguish things that are on the floor, to begin with, but such a big area will take a lot of time to search.

Battalion 9 Chief John O'Rourke, who is the sector chief for this area, comes up with the idea to form a line of firemen across the whole burned-out area. Each of us is an arm's length from the man next to him. We'll walk slowly from the Seventh Avenue side toward the Broadway side, trying to find the missing man.

The line is formed with truckmen and Rescue 1. We are on the right side of the line. Chief O'Rouke is on the far right, Bill Riley is next to him, and I'm next to Bill; the rest of the Rescue and truckmen are on my left.

It is dark and dirty work, just walking and probing along. We move slowly through everything that is incinerated. You can just about make out the man next to you. We are in the area that had been the sporting goods department, which is known to be the point of origin of this fire.

As we slowly move along, Chief O'Rourke suddenly says, "Here's his axe."

The axe is laying against a wainscoated wood partition on the far right of our line. We all move a couple of more steps and I hear Bill Riley say matter-of-factly, "Here he is." I instinctively step to Riley's side, where he's got his light on the form of a firefighter, with all his fire clothing intact, his Scott Air Pack is on his back. He is lying on his stomach, with his upper torso on a low six-inch-high step that is at the bottom of a partition, just like the one where the axe was found, but 10 feet further down and at a right angle from it. He is lying about 10 feet from the corner of the "L"-shaped partition. The facepiece of his mask is half up on his face, probably knocked there when he fell.

Immediately, I kneel down to check him for life. He is completely whole and easily identifiable. He is hot to the touch and I know right away that he is dead. His skin feels like cardboard. I feel death came very fast to him, early on. I give a cursory look at his air bottle gauge, but I don't come to a conclusion because the plastic cover is gone and the gauge face is blackened, so I can't read it.

The fireman has a name now and as it turns out he is the young truckman we saw at 24 Truck's quarters just a couple of hours ago. He is Walter Smith, a two-year man in the job.

This is a sobering experience for all firemen and it is the thing that leaves most of them with a great sense of mortality and a very definite appreciation for life.

Danny Killoran, the Rescue chauffeur, brings in a Stokes Navy basket. We remove Walter Smith's Scott Air Pak so we can put him in the basket litter that we will bring him out in.

He is a big man. We place him in the Stokes and cover him with a blanket. Then we carry him through the fire door into the adjacent Broadway side of Macy's that was undamaged. Father Julian, the Franciscan priest, is there. He is a much-loved chaplain who lives in the rectory of Saint Francis of Assisi Church, across the street from 24 Truck. Father Julian comes in to the firehouse for a cup of coffee once in a while or comes over to say goodnight to the boys in 24 Truck and Engine 1. He probably already knows Walter Smith very well.

We are waiting for the doctor to come and pronounce death. Father Julian prays while we all kneel around Walter Smith lying in the Stokes basket. I am at his head and it is a very moving scene: dirt-smeared, sweaty, exhausted firemen, quietly kneeling beside their fallen brother.

The doctor comes and I can tell this is not something he has done before. He checks Walter and certifies that he is dead. It is decided that Rescue 1 will take Walter's body to the morgue at Bellevue Hospital. Members of Ladder 24 and Rescue 1 carry Walter Smith's body down to Thirty-Fourth Street, where the rescue rig waits.

The ride to Bellevue Hospital on First Avenue is somber and the men are quiet and reflective of all that has occurred this afternoon. We all feel this is our duty, as well as an honor, to be able to do this for our dead brother.

Upon getting to the morgue, we are brought back out of our grief by just how routine things are there. There is nobody waiting there for us and we have to hunt somebody down to tell us where to go. It appears there is only one person there and this is just another body being brought in as far as he is concerned.

We get inside and he tells us that Walter's clothes have to be removed. I'm sure this is highly unusual, but we do it without reservation. We have to remove his fire clothing and work clothes. He is a big man and he is still warm to the touch due to the heat that killed him.

It is a small comfort that he is not burned and basically looks like he is asleep. That is the way he looks as we leave.

We have Walter's clothing, so we bring it back to the quarters of 24 Truck. There are a lot of people there on the apparatus floor. This is also the Headquarters of the 3rd Division Chief for all of mid-town Manhattan, so this is where the hubbub of the preliminary investigation and inquiry is taking place. It is informal and very similar to a gathering of family members upon the death of a much-loved member.

In the middle of all this, quietly standing off to the side, is the young lieutenant of 24 Truck, who was with Walter Smith moments before his death. Whether he is shocky or not, he looks it to me. Someone has said he's scheduled for an overtime tour tonight. He's in no shape to work tonight and he won't.

Bill Riley and I walk over to him and it's my turn to grab his arm. I say, "Lieutenant, I want you to know that you were the only person on that floor insisting your man was in there." I don't know if this is any comfort or not, but I want him to know this.

As things turn out, though we don't realize it at the time, this lieutenant and I have met before and our paths will cross many times in our FDNY careers.

CHAPTER 10

Connections

There are about 10 of us firefighters and officers sitting on the roof of a burned-out, Lower East Side, six-story tenement. The fire on the upper floor was a tough one and that's why Rescue 1 is still here. The sun isn't even up yet, but we can tell it is going to be a beautiful summer day.

There are members of 18 Truck here, as well as a couple of guys from other companies along with us Rescue guys. Unknown to me at this time, Marty Celic of Ladder 18 is one of the men sitting here on the roof, taking a breather with the rest of us.

This is July 10, 1977, and Marty Celic will work an overtime day tour in Engine Company 15 and I will work an overtime day tour in Rescue 1.

In the early afternoon, Rescue 1 is at a fourth alarm for a pier fire on the Upper West Side at around Sixtieth Street. It is an enormous abandoned pier. It is "going merrily," as we sometimes call a fire that is out of control. It has reached the point of surround and drown, which is not normally FDNY style, but it is just going to take a lot of water and will probably partly burn itself out.

The rescue company is being used like all the other truck companies, helping engines get large-caliber streams in place. While doing this, back-to-back multiple alarms come over the radio for Box 44-439 on East Eighth Street.

Lieutenant Richie Bittles is the officer covering today in Rescue 1. It is his first time here and we all like him. Before we ever hear it said that there are firemen trapped, we know there is a problem due to how fast the multiple alarms come in. The lieutenant asks Battalion Chief Grimes of the 9th Battalion if we can be released to try to aid the firefighters who are trapped on East Eighth Street on the Lower East Side. Without hesitation, Chief Grimes releases us. Besides being a very experienced fire officer, he is a reserve Marine Corps colonel.

When we get down to East Eighth Street, we see that Rescue 2 has come from Brooklyn and they are standing by. The men of Engine 15 who were trapped had gotten out, but one of them, Marty Celic, had jumped to the tower ladder bucket and slipped and fallen in the heavy, blinding smoke. He will die as a result of his injuries.

Rescue 2 has arrived here before us, but not in time to help the men who were trapped. They are standing by as rescue crews sometimes do when not immediately needed until the fire is under control.

The Rescue crew members are standing together and I'm standing next to this friendly fireman from Rescue 2. He tells me what he knows of what has transpired before we arrived. He normally works in the group of Lieutenant Bobby Babstock, who happens to be one of my best friends in the fire department. Bobby and I were very good friends in Ladder 102, and he was a wonderful, tough truckman.

This fireman from Rescue 2 with the pleasant and easy-going manner is Pete Hayden. We will part and will not see each other again until he comes out of that awful fifth-floor doorway at Macy's Department store, almost two years later, as a new lieutenant.

Sometime after the fire at Macy's, Bobby Babstock was promoted to captain, and Rescue 2 gave a party in his honor. Pete Hayden was there and I had a chance to reintroduce myself to him. At Macy's, we did not recognize each other or realize we had met before.

Because the Macy's fire was a while ago, I felt I could ask his opinion of what had happened when he and 24 Truck responded there. Apparently, about 15 minutes before Engine 1 and 24 Truck, the first due companies, got there, some employees had attempted to put a fire out in the back storeroom of the sports department on the fifth floor. It overwhelmed them and they notified the fire department. On entering the area, Pete and the men could see the televisions on in the electronics department and not much evidence of smoke. At the origin of the fire, there were expended extinguishers from the futile civilian attempts. As they got to the storeroom, there was a massive smoke explosion or flashover in the six-foot-high space above the high store ceiling. This occurs when there's an accumulation of heat, oxygen, and hot gases such as carbon monoxide. The explosion blew some of the ceiling down with sudden heat and fire. From experience, Pete knew the only way out was to go back to the main aisle and backtrack the way they came in. This is always a procedure in large areas. To Walter Smith, who had two years in the fire department, it may have looked like they were going into the worst of it. Pete had Walter Smith by the sleeve when Smith broke away to what he might have thought was a short cut to the door. If there was visibility, it would look like that path could be taken. But when there suddenly was no visibility, with the store partitions in this area, it could and did become a trap for the young fireman.

At moments like this, there is hardly enough time to think and it comes down to experience, as well as instinct. Things got so very bad so suddenly that there wasn't any way that Lieutenant Hayden could go after his man at this moment. Pete Hayden's words to me were that he saw "the curtain of death" before him. That was the cause of the initial commotion and rolling out of the door to the landing that we witnessed that fateful day.

One can only conjecture about what Walter Smith was trying to do to save himself. Under the circumstances, this is something that could happen to anyone faced with running for his or her life.

On September 11, 2001, Assistant Chief Pete Hayden would be in command at the Command Post at the South Tower of the World Trade Center after the attack. Later, he would become the Chief of Department to succeed Chief of Department Pete Ganci, who was killed on 9/11 along with Deputy Commissioner Bill Feehan.

After the Macy's fire, I would work with Al Fuentes in Rescue 1, who was one of the men who came out the door that day as a member of 24 Truck. We would become good friends and become part of the same study group for promotion to lieutenant. He would become a lieutenant in Ladder 102 and then Rescue 2. As a captain in the Marine Division, he would respond to the World Trade Center on 9/11, where he would be trapped under debris and be one of the few rescued. He would write his book, "American by Choice" about his fight for survival.

CHAPTER 11

September 1979—A Night with the Pope

Tom Baldwin had been a fireman and lieutenant in Rescue 1. This tall, angular, and deceivingly big man, born in Ireland, became the captain of Rescue 1.

Bill Siegel, who would eventually be a deputy chief, and I were discussing what it was like working with Tom Baldwin, who was such a fearless, hard-driving man at a fire. He was a big man with a lot of energy. Consequently, when you worked with him, you covered a lot of ground and were forced to work as hard as he did. He definitely led by example and his force of personality and common decency would not let you do otherwise. Bill hit it right on the head when he said, "Working with Tom Baldwin was like working with your favorite uncle."

Captain Baldwin calls me at home in September of 1979. He asks me if I want to work a night tour of overtime. I'm just getting over a cold, but it's a tour of overtime. He says, "You're going to work in Harlem." It's busy up there and I know it will probably be an exciting night. Despite my fraction of a second's reservation, I tell him, "Yes." He says, "Are you sure?" It'll be a tough night, but I tell him, "Yes." Then he says to me, "You're going to guard the Pope." It would turn out to be an exciting night all right, but not the way I thought originally.

Dan Killoran, a good friend, is the other man I'll be with that night. We will stay at the Cardinal's Residence in back of St. Patrick's Cathedral on the corner of Madison Avenue and East Fiftieth Street.

This is not a usual detail for a fireman, although it's more likely to occur here in Manhattan than in other parts of the city. The reason that Danny and I are going to stay at Cardinal Cook's Residence is that Pope John Paul II was going to stay there while in New York, as part of his visit to America.

The Cardinal's Residence is a three-story, stone, colonial-style structure, with a foyer that's opened to the third floor. This is the private residence of the Cardinal, so the structure is traditional and open and not subject to fire codes for public buildings. With such an eminence as the Pope staying there, it has been determined that a fire watch should be there to guard him. The Pope is going to stay overnight after saying Mass at Yankee Stadium.

Danny and I report to the 8th Battalion on East Fifty-First Street in our "Class A" uniforms. We have a Scott Air-Pak for each of us, forcible entry tools, and fire extinguishers. At about 8:00 p.m., the battalion chief drives us over to the Cardinal's Residence.

In front of the Cardinal's Residence is a cordon of uniformed police officers going right up the front steps. We are escorted up the stairs to the front door with all our gear, where we are met by a Monsignor, who we understand to be the Cardinal's secretary. As we go in, there are two rooms off to the right of the foyer. There is a large front window in each room. The first room is the secretary's, so he takes us to the next room, where we will be ensconced with our tools.

At this time, there are no police officers in the building. Throughout the night, Danny and I will be the only uniformed people in residence. Shortly after our arrival, a member of the Secret Service interviews us. The Secret Service personnel are mostly all in the rectory, which also is in back of St. Patrick's Cathedral, but on the corner of Madison Avenue and East Fifty-First Street. It's a symmetrical building to the Cardinal's Residence we are in.

The Secret Service man, who checks out who we are and what our function is, indicates that the Secret Service would like us to stay with them in the other building. However, the whole reason for our being here is to be near the Pope in residence. We will remain here.

Maura is the very efficient head of the house staff. She is from Ireland and speaks with a brogue as she introduces herself to us. This is obviously a busy time for her, but there is probably a fireman on her family tree somewhere. No matter how busy she is, she manages to look in on us from time to time to make sure we're comfortable. She's all business with everyone, but seems to have a soft spot for us. I guess she senses she can be a little more casual with us and she is right.

As the evening moves on, in anticipation of the Pope's arrival, there is a pair of plainclothes police officers sitting on a small reception bench across the foyer. One of them is a New York detective and the other is with the Secret Service.

Maura comes to get Danny and me to show us where Pope John Paul II will sleep. This is a privilege that no one else will have, except for the Pope's entourage.

The couple of rooms for the Pope and his closest people are on the third floor, directly above us. Maura takes us into what will be the Pope's bedroom. I am taken with how austere it all is. The single bed has a simple white bedcover and there is no headboard. There is a small crucifix on the wall at the head of the bed.

There is good reason for us to see where the Pope will be during the night. We also know which window is closest to him, in case we have to get to him by ladder from outside.

We are back in our room when Maura comes in and tells us that we need beds. We are not thinking of sleep tonight with all the excitement the Pope's visit is causing around us. Danny tells her that we don't need beds. She insists, so I offer to go with her to help. There is an elevator in the foyer that goes down to the cellar. We go down to a storage area, where she finds a rollaway cot. We put it on the elevator to the first floor foyer and I back out, pulling the cot behind me, Maura pushing.

I can sense the eyes of the New York detective and the Secret Service man on me, wondering what is going on. Anticipating what they may be thinking, I say, "You know a fireman can't do a night tour without a bed."

One bed is enough because Danny insists that he won't be able to sleep. More than likely, I won't either. At this time, there is much anticipation of the Pope's arrival.

Madison Avenue between East Fiftieth and East Fifty-First streets is mobbed with people who have come to see the Pope's arrival here. Many will stay all night as a vigil to the Pope's presence.

Around 11:00 p.m., the din of the crowd on the street rises to extreme excitement. Pope John Paul II is arriving.

There is a small hallway that connects the two rooms on our side to the foyer. We walk down to the foyer, and we can see the Pope on the top of the stairs greeting all the well-wishers in the street. Danny is standing in front of me and says, "There he is." Danny is Irish Catholic and this is an emotional, as well as momentous, experience.

The Pope says his good-night to the crowd in the street and there is the sound of the barred metal front door being opened. John Paul II takes the couple of steps up to the foyer, where we are and turns again toward outside. He is radiant-looking. Many leaders look fit and are nice-looking in person. This is more so. It is early in his papacy and he is just a couple of years into his sixties. He is handsome, sturdy, and robust-looking. He's all in white and I am sure it adds to the image. He has a halo about him. Later, I will hear the term "La Bella Figura"—The Beautiful Image—and I believe that is what we are seeing. Maybe that's what Attila the Hun saw when he met the Pope in the river and was turned around.

There is an entourage of church hierarchy with the Pope, but they are not inside yet. The only people in the foyer are the two plainclothes men across from us, Danny Killoran, me, and the Pope.

September 1979—A Night with the Pope

Danny and I are in full dress uniform, jackets on, and hatless. It is a benefit because our uniforms may have caught Pope John Paul II's attention. Before anyone else is inside, he turns toward us and momentarily looks as if he is focusing his eyes on us, wondering who we are. Without hesitation, he comes over to us at the side of the foyer. Danny is still in front of me and when the Pope gets to him, Danny genuflects, takes the Pope's hand, and kisses his ring. I can tell the charge of love and emotion by the flush on the back of Danny's ears and neck.

Next, the Pope comes to me and I am caught up in the extraordinary moment also. I am Lutheran, but I recognize the Pope as the leader of the Christian world. I also take the Pope's hand while looking into his eyes in that wonderful face. I say to him, "God Bless You." He brings his head toward me, nose to nose, looking deep into my eyes and says in a deep, low solemn tone, "God Bless You." It is an extremely moving moment for me.

Pope John Paul II moves smoothly and quickly to the New York detective and Secret Service man across the foyer. This has all happened before the people traveling with him have come in.

The Pope has two Vatican policemen with him and two Swiss Guards. They suddenly appear and whisk him away to the back of the foyer and upstairs. As he leaves, it is as if someone turned off the lights. His Holiness looks suddenly tired, with somewhat less radiance than we witnessed when he came in, saying goodnight to the people outside and greeting and blessing us.

Just as this all happens, the entourage of red-sashed clergymen comes inside. As the Cardinal's secretary closes the wrought iron outside door, Danny and I move back toward our room and I hear the Monsignor ask the church leaders, "Gentlemen, would anyone like a libation?" It's been a long trip from Yankee Stadium to midtown Manhattan with the leader of the Catholic Church and the whole Christian world. This is a civil, worldly moment after a long day.

The Pope is already in his room on the third floor, and I sense a certain informal relaxation in the house. Almost right away, the Cardinal's secretary, the Monsignor, comes in and graciously offers us something to drink. A beer would taste good, but we dutifully ask for soda. Shortly after the Monsignor leaves, a tray with two magnificent crystal goblets of clear soda is brought to us.

I'm astonished at the weight of the goblets and look underneath the stem and base to identify something about them. Danny admonishes me, kidding, "George, you can't take that." I allay his unfounded fears.

Sometime around midnight, Maura comes in to ask if we need anything and to bid us goodnight. She will see us in the morning. The house is going to sleep.

Through the night, we have free run of the whole first floor. From time to time, I wander around the living room and dining area where the Pope will have breakfast before saying Mass in the cathedral later this morning. There are many tasteful artifacts around on the various antique tables. They are gifts to the Cardinal or the archdiocese from many notables in New York society.

The galley in the cellar is open to us throughout the night, for coffee, tea, and snacks. There are a couple of newly ordained St. Patrick's priests who look after things down there.

For a break and an excuse to move around, I go down to the cellar galley to have a cup of coffee. The Secret Service man is down there. He is a midwestern Protestant and he is engaged in a very interesting, high-level discussion with one of the priests about what it means to be in the service of the Pope, protecting him. It just presses home the honor I already feel by being here. It is said that those who guard the Pope on earth will be with him in heaven. If this one night of guarding the Pope deserves only a little candle, I will be happy with that.

All is quiet in the house. Even the first floor galley for the dining room across the hall from us has its lights out. It is well past midnight and everything is hushed and peaceful.

We have this cot taking up a lot of the space in our small office room. Danny is not an excitable person, but he is not going to use this cot this night. Even the crowd in the street on cordoned off Madison Avenue has lightened slightly and it is fairly quiet there.

About 4:00 a.m., I decide not to waste the cot that Maura forced on us. I take my shoes off and fade, only to have Maura come cheerily into the room at 5:00 a.m. to let us know the day has begun. She draws back the curtains and wishes us good morning. As a fireman on duty, I am instantly awake.

Outside. there is the most beautiful caroling I have ever heard. Female voices, male voices, and mixtures, all coming from different quarters of the street. To call it magnificent does not do it justice. John Paul II is definitely being serenaded with what I imagine are the sounds of heaven.

We look out the window and look upon a sea of Roman collars of priests and habits of nuns. Five o'clock in the morning and the street is packed with people and the most joyous singing.

It doesn't take long for things to come alive in the house. Caterers from the Waldorf–Astoria have come in like a dawning whirlwind to prepare breakfast for a Pope. They have completely taken over the cellar galley and have gone right to work, with no wasted motion.

Daylight comes and there is a lot of activity in the dining room galley across from us. There is this very fit-looking middle-aged man, with a noticeably amiable and charming way about him, talking pleasantly with the ladies who are busy preparing the breakfast dining table for the Pope, Cardinal Cook, and guests. He is a mid-sized man with an athletic and military bearing. His look is Italian–Swiss and his countenance is confident and friendly. Danny says he thinks he is Swiss Guard.

After the activity of the breakfast table preparation simmers down, this nattily dressed man in well-fitted civilian suit and tie comes into our room, accompanied by a similarly dressed, big, serious-looking man, who is the size of a big heavyweight fighter and just as fit. The smaller

Swiss Guard leads the way and exclaims in a loud voice, "THE FIREMEN." In Italy, there is tremendous love and respect for their firemen. This comes through in his greeting.

Danny asks him if he is Swiss Guard. He says he is. Then Danny says, "I thought all Swiss Guards were very tall?" He unreservedly answers, "Yes, they are two meters high, but I'm the major and I guess I'm the one," meaning the short one. He is around five-nine or five-ten. So I say to him, while motioning with my hand that we are eye to eye, "In the Rescue, where I come from, I'm the one." He really likes this and he shakes my hand vigorously.

The affable major of the Swiss Guard is the boss and he tells his companion to give us gifts. The gifts are a medallion commemorating the 1979 visit to America by Pope John Paul II. His likeness is on one side and the Papal Seal is on the other. They give us each rosary beads and the major says, "Give them more." The Vatican policeman obeys, reaching in his pocket to give us more. These small gifts are of little intrinsic value, but they are cherished as if they were.

The two soldiers go off to bestow gifts on staff people throughout the house. As they breeze through, the major is so charming that at every stop he makes, we can hear the life and cheer he brings with him.

Eventually, activity in the front of the house becomes fairly routine, while the Pope, Cardinal, and other Church leaders and guests have breakfast. After about an hour, the breakfast entourage congregates in the foyer. Danny and I stand in the hallway to the side. Pope John Paul II moves around the perimeter greeting and blessing the house staff. We stay back. One blessing was enough for a lifetime.

The Pope has brought gifts for his host, Cardinal Cook, and for St. Patrick's Catherdral. They are in large, wooden, banded shipping crates. Everyone is there to see the opening of the gifts.

The Swiss Guard major is in charge of the opening and sees that there is a problem with cutting the bands on the crates. He is deep in the middle of the group, looking for assistance and makes eye contact with us, as if we were who he was looking for. He can see immediately that we are anxious to help him. He smiles and makes a hand signal, indicating he is looking for something to cut with. He must know all firemen carry a sharp knife. I hold up my folded pocketknife, which I proudly keep as sharp as a razor. The major takes it and cuts all the bands and then gratefully returns it with a big smile.

They encounter another little problem of opening the nailed-down lids. It is Danny's turn to step out into the middle of the foyer with the Halligan tool and he pries open the lids. To be able to help with the most simple things, to us, is a big deal and an honor.

The gifts are sacramental objects that include religious, beautifully decorated six-foot candles for St. Patrick's Cathedral.

After the presentation, the Pope walks out the front door to the front steps to greet the throng in the street. The cheer that comes up from the crowd is unbelievable.

Across Madison Avenue, there is a duplex mansion, with ironwork going up behind it, to be attached to it. This will eventually be the Helmsley Palace Hotel. The ironworkers have hung banners from the iron/steel structure that say "Ironworkers Love John Paul II," "New York Welcomes the Pope," "God bless Pope John Paul II," and so on. The love being spirited across Madison Avenue both ways is something to behold.

After all this adulation, Pope John Paul II goes through the house to the back of St. Patrick's Cathedral to say Mass. He will leave directly from there.

Everyone leaves and there is just the staff and us two firemen left. Maura, the head of the staff, insists we have breakfast from the Pope's table. They put together a wonderful breakfast for Danny and me that includes kielbasa, from the Polish Pope's table.

The greatest detail of our lives was just about over. This would define us for the rest of our careers as "the Firemen who spent the night with the Pope."

As we are thanking Maura for everything and taking our leave, we notice a little Italian man carrying down these huge, heavy pieces of baggage. We help him, and they are incredibly heavy, as if everything the Pope owned was in them. This old man is about 75 years old and he is very thankful. We can't believe he was carrying these down himself. We bid him goodbye. He is the Pope's valet and physician.

CHAPTER 12

Attempt at a Diary—102 Truck

Friday, January 31, 1969
9:10 a.m., Box 22-270, Bushwick Avenue and McKibbin Street

My first fire as a member of Ladder Co. 102. We are not assigned on the alarm box card. Because Ladder 108 is at another box, we request duty at this fire. We are assigned above the fire. After trying interior stairs, I find them fully involved with fire, and engines, including my former company, Engine 230, are hard at work. Lieutenant Ronnie Browne, a former Marine, Hank Gmelin, a young former Marine who had served in Vietnam, and I proceed to the rear fire escape through an apartment below the fire. We help many adults and small children down the fire escape to safety. After all of them are safe, we force entry to all apartments on our designated side above the fire. On our side, on the third of six floors, two children, ages two and three years, are killed in the fire apartment. This was an arson fire.

Monday, February 10, 1969
9:48 a.m., Box 55-623, Greene Avenue and Clermont Street

A church fire (75 feet by 150 feet) that went on to a fifth alarm.
After the 20-inch snow blizzard of the day before, most streets are blocked. Ladder 102, assigned on the third alarm, responds on the second alarm. We are the first truck company to get to the fire building

with the apparatus, a 1962 American La France. This rig is a tractor–trailer with a tiller. There are times the tractor is going sideways at snow-clogged intersections and around corners. Luckily, we have the night crew as well as the day crew. We all get off the rig and push the tractor of the truck until we get traction again. This is done several times, enabling us to get there.

We operate the ladder pipe for four hours. There has been a delayed alarm and when we get there the roof is at the point of collapse. It is freezing cold and miserable. The priests and brothers who teach at Bishop Loughlin High School nearby have been watching the progress of the fire on the frozen street. During the fire operations, they make a hot bacon and egg breakfast for all of us firemen. They serve us in their teachers' dining hall with its tables for four. We all remove our wet boots and fire clothing and leave them at the door to this warm dining room. We eat, relaxed, in our stockinged feet. The priests and brothers serve us cheerfully with great hospitality.

Tuesday, February 11, 1969
8:10 p.m., 2010 Box 55-678, Marcy and Green avenues, St. Augustine's Episcopal Church

Fully involved church fire when we get in, first due. Charlie Stressler, the chauffeur, uses the aerial ladder to vent the beautiful front rose window. We force the front doors of the church and have to abandon that position.

We proceed to make preliminary searches of the exposed tenement building next door. We evacuate the entire building because there is a tremendously hot fire, a second alarm, that has come across the airshaft into two whole floors. We spend 13 hours, cold and miserable, at this location.

The aerial ladder is almost lost from fire and danger of the front wall falling on it.

March 5, 1969
4:00 p.m., Box 33-672, Myrtle and Marcy avenues

First due truck at a third alarm new law tenement, six stories, front and rear apartments. I have forcible entry, axe and Halligan tool. Working to force a door of the top floor, front left, fire having burned through from the floor below, comes out in a ball of fire, driving firemen into the rear apartments. I dive down the stairway, off the landing.

CHAPTER 13

Pete Cusumano: A Firefighter

As I make my way to the second flight of stairs, there is the distinct aroma of sautéed peppers and onions mingled with the evident summer evening air working its way through the open window and doors. In the dimness of the second floor, I can see the 16 army-type bunks not too heavily used in this particular neighborhood. Taking the hundred-year-old wooden stairs two at a time, I get to the third-floor landing, which had been the living quarters of the Brooklyn Fire Department fire captain and his family in post–Civil War days. Now, it is used as a locker room and kitchen. The rows of lockers divide the front of the floor, with its pool table and open windows, from the back, which is used as a kitchen. Through the open windows of the back I can hear the city sounds mixed with an occasional barking backyard dog and the ever-present sound of the children at play.

Walking back toward the kitchen, I can hear the conversations of men coming on duty and those going off. They are mostly seated at the large banquet table drinking coffee, those going off filling in the men just coming in on the day's events. It is around six o'clock; despite the sound of distant sirens, the atmosphere is momentarily relaxed.

At the stove is the source of the pepper and onion aroma. Sautéeing the preparation for peppers and eggs is a stockily built, well-mustached Italian-American type. He is in a T-shirt with a dish towel around his neck in the fashion of a neckerchief; his curly hair forms ringlets down the middle of his forehead, the result of the perspiration of his labor.

These are the quarters of Engine Company 235 and Squad Company 3, Fire Department, New York, located on Monroe Street in Bedford-Stuyvesant, and these are among the busiest companies in the city. Just a year before, Squad 3 had lost one of its members when a section of a 14-foot-high ceiling in a hundred-year-old school had pancaked on top of the whole working crew. Out of six members, two are still on the job, one was killed, and three suffered various disabilities.

I am detailed to Engine 235 from my own Engine 230, my turn having come up for a month's stay. Engine 235 is low on manpower and my own company is supplying a man a month from its own roster. Engine 230 is one block north of Myrtle Avenue, making it a Williamsburg company, while Engine 235 is housed smack in the middle of Bedford-Stuyvesant.

Summertime Bed-Stuy brings people out of their steamy homes and onto the hot pavement of the city streets. People sit on stoops talking over a can of beer or hanging out windows to escape the heat or to see what excitement the night might bring. Noisy children play and chase each other around the street. Rows of brownstones with their high parlor-floor stoops are interspersed with the occasional private frame house that has long left the hands of the solid middle-class people who formerly lived there. This is the neighborhood Pete Cusumano and the rest of us choose to work in.

At this time, Pete has about five years in the job and he has already changed companies by going across the floor from Engine 235 to Squad 3, probably figuring that the transfer would bring him more action. Squad 3, besides having its own large response area, responds to most greater alarm fires where manpower is needed.

As a man who works hard at making other people comfortable, with a ready and easy smile and the willingness to do more than his share in the firehouse, it isn't at all evident that as a younger man he had been so two-fisted that, it is said, he carried a rubber mouthpiece on him just in case a fistfight broke out. Nor can one see any hardness from his experiences as an infantryman in Korea in the softness of his dark brown eyes. The only outward sign of toughness is in the ruggedness of his peasant-type face and the solidness of the body that might have turned less hard on someone else of the same age and body type.

Pete is always in the kitchen cooking a meal to satisfy the troops; often it's an Italian meal with sauce—countless times it's his peppers and eggs. He always gives one hundred percent at a fire as well as in the kitchen.

I get to know him a little in my one-month stay in Engine 235, but it isn't until two years later, when Squad 3 moves to the quarters of Engine 230, that I get to know him better.

Squad companies fluctuate between the duties of an engine that puts the fire out and a truck or ladder company that ladders and ventilates burning buildings of heated gases and smoke. So there are times that I see Pete as part of a team moving a handline and attacking the fire or on the roof ventilating it by opening it up by its vertical openings or helping to get people down the rear fire escapes or down ladders to safety.

In 1969, I transfer to Ladder Company 102, which is referred to on the job as 102 Truck. Having individual assignments to cover all parts of the building, a truckman may have the job of roof ventilation on one day and forcible entry to the fire floor on another, or may perform the necessary laddering of the front or rear of the building involved.

It is as a truckman that I actually get to see more of Pete at fires. Often, we have parallel jobs at fires and if we don't, we cross paths in the course of the battle. It doesn't matter what he is doing at a particular time, it's sure that he is always in the thick of things. Always fully involved in what he is doing, he takes more than his share of risks and punishment. Because he extends himself with such aggressiveness and initiative, he wins the respect of all who come in contact with him. The image of Pete, thoroughly exhausted and recuperating after most jobs, lingers.

One night, we respond to an 80-year-old frame house that has at least 10 families living in it. There isn't a lick of paint left on the original clapboard that sheaths it, making the building a potential tinderbox. We are there because a drunk insisted on trying to set fire to the building full of people. He has a large family of his own living there also. There isn't much work involved in dousing the small building fire. However, we have to search the building to see if this guy has set any more fires in the building. Then we wait for the police to arrive to apprehend the drunken arsonist.

This is Williamsburg, where a fireman can get very used to somebody intentionally torching a building full of people. But, as we are hanging around the truck outside the building, waiting for the police, Pete comes over to a couple of us standing near the rumbling trucks, to point out two of the apartments that have around 10 kids in each of them. He doesn't know these people at all, but his interest is far deeper than the placard- or bandwagon-type or only of a professional nature. As he explains the layouts of the apartments and the location of the kids, one has only to look into his eyes to see the compassion of a man who cares deeply about the welfare of other human beings.

In June 1971, we take the test for promotion to lieutenant. Six thousand guys take the test on this day in different schools around the city. Men from our area of work take the test at Brooklyn Technical High School. Coincidentally, Pete and I wind up in the same room. Pete, the anxiety evident on his face, sits among us in the rows of school desks, waiting for the proctor to come in with the four-hour examination of 100 questions. The examination can never reflect the amount of study, anguish, and time away from the family that a man puts himself through in preparation. Not all of us have given it the effort it requires, but Pete has. He's put in a couple of years of studying for hours every day; despite this, he takes the time to wink good luck to those of us who deserve to make it so much less than he does.

Well, most of us either don't pass or pass with too low a mark to ever be made lieutenant, but Pete passes with a mark in the high 80s; with his points from citations tacked on, he earns a place on the top part of the promotion list of around a thousand. It appears that he might even be made lieutenant soon enough to take the captain's exam.

There has been a delay in the certification of the lists so, in the summer of '72, Pete is still getting his head knocked in with the rest of us grunts. One hot day when fires are erupting all over the borough, every man in Squad 3 and Engine 230 suffers smoke inhalation and heat exhaustion. I am sent over to their quarters as a replacement for those knocked out at the fire. The replacements are from all over and the crews that have been felled at the fire are waiting for the fire department doctor to arrive to examine them.

Having lived in this place for five years myself, the first thing I do upon arrival is to seek out old friends. The temperature is in the stifling 90s, so a lot of the men are in the backyard, sitting on anything they can find, sipping some well-deserved liquid refreshment. In a corner of the yard sits Pete with a cold can in his hand, with his face blackened with dirt and soot and his curly hair matted down from the leather helmet. Resembling a miner after a day's work, his clothes soaked through with perspiration, he is the very embodiment of the thoroughly spent firefighter. He calls me over for a drink and a little friendly shoptalk. He is sitting on a milk box against the brick back wall of a garage that juts onto the firehouse yard. We talk about the fire that brutalized them on this hotter than normal day. The conversation gets to his imminent promotion to lieutenant and his chances of making it in time for the captain's exam. He is high enough to make it still possible. The thought of that eventuality shows in the brightness that grins through the dirt and sweat of his rugged, toothy face. I am looking at a man who knows he does his job well and loves being in the company of others he regards in the same light. In back of those smiling eyes is the certainty that he deserves the upcoming promotion and will handle being the captain of his own company quite easily when that day arrives. I start calling him "Captain Cusumano."

I see Pete from time to time, most often passing him on stairs or hallways getting from one place in the fire building to another—always where the action is and always extending himself a little further. Consequently, one night in late September, Pete and other members of the squad are attacking a stubborn inferno on the third floor of a burning frame tenement, when the fire, having suddenly gotten ventilation, blows out the apartment door. The men are forced into a quick retreat, bounding over railings and down the stairwell to form a cluster of tangled bodies at the bottom. Outside of the routine aches and pain that accompany this type of thing, the firefighters appear to be none the worse for their momentary withdrawal. Untangling themselves from their predicament, they are able to rally themselves into an organized advance on the fire.

Later, Pete complains of neck and back discomfort from the plunge down the stairs. He is examined by a fire department doctor and found to be in good enough condition to go home and rest on his break until his next tour of duty. He is back to work on October 2, although some of his friends think it is too soon. His only complaint is of his sore knees, the result of landing on the stairs. After reporting this, Pete continues on full duty status until the morning of October 24. At this time, Pete's wife contacts his good friend and lieutenant, Pete Carino, and tells him that her husband is unusually sick. Lieutenant Carino has a fire department ambulance dispatched to take the stricken fireman to Coney Island Hospital for examination. They are unable to diagnose the problem, so Pete Carino personally takes him to Brooklyn Hospital, where they determine he has suffered a cerebral hemorrhage or stroke.

It isn't long before Pete is brought to Rusk Institute for rehabilitation and further observation. Some of the men who get to see him at this critical time are overwhelmed by his almost complete incapacitation. He has almost complete paralysis—except for his eyes, he is pretty much unresponsive. This later smoothes out to a right-side paralysis. The guys who visit him can't be sure if he can comprehend their concern and interest.

On a dank and rainy day in November, I go over to see Pete at the Rusk Institute at First Avenue and Thirty-Fourth Street. When I get there, I locate his room on the fourth floor of that center for all forms of debilitation and disabilities. Pete is at a consultation with neurologists, who are trying to decide how they can ameliorate his present situation. Standing in the hall, I see every method of locomotion imaginable. People are wheeled, carried, or otherwise cajoled from one place to another. In about half an hour, Pete is wheeled past me to his room without noticing me—on his face I see a blank look of resignation and an almost complete loss of interest in his surroundings.

Walking up to him when he is settled in his room, still seated in the wheelchair, he's momentarily slow to recognize me. Then there is the realization and acknowledgment in his eyes.

"Hi Pete!" I say. He gives me a shrug of half and half. He's evidently glad to see me, but this once notably confident man is not comfortable having a visitor in that environment.

It is obvious that he can comprehend what is said to him but has trouble giving more than yes or no responses. He has to ponder momentarily my questions about how he is doing. It is easier for me to hold a one-way conversation with him and then let him acknowledge with a nod of yes or shake of no. At least he is better off than he had been when some of the guys had seen him a couple of weeks earlier. He is able to hobble onto his bed from the wheelchair. We talk about the rainy, early winter weather and about ships that can be seen docked or navigating up and down the East River. I try to indicate how little he is missing at work while still feeling the tightness of my own chest from smoke feeds from the night before. I don't know if it is disinterest or just that he is decidedly cognizant of the fact that there is something back in the firehouse that he will never be a part of again.

After about an hour of visiting, I decide to leave because he has another consultation scheduled for this afternoon. I can still picture him as he lies there, probably thinking of the upcoming consultation and its results. As he lies there in slacks and a knit shirt, with his limp right arm supported in a sling, I bid him "So long." Nodding to me, he quickly focuses his eyes on the ceiling and his thoughts inward.

Stepping out into the rain and the heavy traffic of First Avenue, I think, "I'll have to get back up here in another week or two."

On Thursday, December 7, Fireman 1st Grade Peter Cusumano, age 40, dies as a result of an embolus that originated as a clot after his knee injuries. There is lingering disbelief, mostly because we just expect a strong individual like that to recover.

Pete's wake is held in an area of Brooklyn where he grew up. Firefighters who have known Pete at one time or another come to pay their respects from all over the city. These and still others will attend his funeral later on. Due to the relative hazards of a job that requires a man to crawl through blinding, acrid smoke into places he's never been before, there is always more than usual homage paid to a fallen comrade who has shared these experiences. Only other firefighters can understand how one learns to survive while never quite getting used to one's lot.

Lying there, Pete looks more like the warm-hearted, rugged man I had come to know so well. On the open cover of the casket, there's a picture of Pete smiling beneath his leather headpiece, holding a baby he had saved from what would have been imminent death at arm's length above his head. There is the news clipping that accompanied the picture in the local newspapers and a copy of one of his five citations. Next to these is a card from one of his little girls that says, "I am so lucky because I have the best Daddy in the whole world. I love you, Daddy."

Sometimes it's hard to accept the temporary nature of life, even for a fireman who should know better. Standing at the bier, I try to figure what makes life so abrupt. Is it the grievous loss of a fine man and friend? A man makes his mark and passes on. What is it all for?

I look at the picture that is so typical of Pete in his life, the card from his little girl, and the citation. Maybe that is what it is all about.

CHAPTER 14

Boy in the Shaft

It is a beautiful midsummer evening, 1976, just about sunset. The rescue company has just come back from a run and we are about to sit down for our evening meal, which was started and worked on earlier.

The dispatcher special calls us verbally with information that a child is missing in a building near Engine 14 on East Eighteenth Street. That is all we know when we roll into the area of the building. There is a series of big, old, multi-story factory buildings in this area and confusion as to which building the child is or was in.

The first due engine and trucks are searching the labyrinth of partially interconnected, large, complicated buildings. There is a lot of confusion because this alarm came in as a phone call and it's uncertain who called or where the call came from. The motor pump operator of Engine 14 tells us that a small child has supposedly fallen into a vertical shaft way.

As we join the search of the buildings, we begin to realize that these are loft buildings that have become homes to "Artists in Residence." People attracted by the large areas for studios as well as living space are living here.

There are shafts for elevators and light, and airshafts for ventilation—it's not immediately apparent where all of them are. A lot of simultaneous searching is going on by the various engine and truck companies, in addition to Rescue Company 1.

Because there are already other companies combing the buildings, Captain Bill Anderson keeps us all together until we know more of what has already been accomplished by the companies who have arrived before us.

The building in question is confirmed and it just happens to be the building we are already in. A civilian has encountered us inside and tells us he knows what happened and the location of the shaft way.

He leads us through the basement to about the center of the 100 foot by 100 foot, eight-story building. He says there is a small side opening into the bottom of the shaft. I'm five feet ten inches and weigh 160 pounds, which makes me the smallest member of this crew. The captain tells me, "George, I want you to be the first one into that shaft." He is sure I'll fit through the opening and he also knows I've handled many medical and life-threatening emergencies before.

We get to the opening to the shaft and it is small, but not so small that bigger men can't get in with a struggle. I scramble into the bottom of what was probably an airshaft at one time. In the corner of the bottom lies an eight-year-old boy, looking like he is sleeping, with 50 years of dust covering him. He doesn't look real. Lying there, with no sign of a struggle, he looks like a mannequin that has been lying in the dusty shaft for years.

Upon seeing this little boy, I know he is dead, but I check him for life anyway. I tell Captain Anderson that I'm sure he is dead and he sends in Mike Walsh with a body bag in order to get this unfortunate little guy out of there.

Mike and I gently place him in the bag. Just before closing the bag, we are told that the mother and father of the boy want to see him. For us, this is a very unusual occurrence.

With help from firemen outside the shaft, the mother and father crawl into where we are with their son. Mike and I are kneeling next to him in all the dust and debris. We have dusted off his face before his parents see him. It is a touching and tender moment to see. A man holding his wife, tenderly supportive, while she touches her little boy's cheek and brushes the hair from his forehead. She quietly and softly says, "We loved you, Matthew. You were a good boy."

These are very genteel people, who do not belong here in this dirty shaft with their dead little boy. Shortly before, they were a happy, young family on the roof of an eight-story building, watching the end of a beautiful day.

The family had moved from an uptown tenement area to this area so there would be more room for all of them. They were also a little concerned about the safety of their sons with the tenement fire escapes.

The mother and father had taken their two little boys, eight- and nine-year-old brothers, to the roof to watch a lovely sunset and sundown.

As all little boys do, the two were investigating the roof under the watchful gaze of their parents when the younger one fell through the tarred-over glass covering the shaft. There were steel cross members tying the walls of the shaft together. He probably hit some of these on his way down and was killed in a split second. By the looks of him, he was probably already dead when he hit the bottom. His body landed with such force that it raised the dust on the bottom of the shaft so that it covered him evenly like he had been there for years.

The irony of people moving from a place they considered unsafe to another that they believed would be safer, only to have something like this happen, was inescapable. Life may not be fragile and it can be happy, but death can come suddenly.

1958 1000 G.P.M. Mack Pumper.

Photo by Alex Donchin

George R. Kreuscher at work.

Photo by Alex Donchin

Fireman Kreuscher with fire escape hook and Engine 230 getting hoseline up fire escape while Lt. Tom Zuercher waits above.

Photo by Alex Donchin

The way it is sometimes.

Photo by Alex Donchin

George Kreuscher, Engine Company 230.

Photo by Alex Donchin

Squad 3, left to right: Gary Howard, Bill Hayes, Lt. Hank Zuercher, Pete Cusumano.

George Kreuscher of Ladder Company 102.

Classic brownstone fire.

Photo by Alex Donchin

Newspaper coverage.

Long Island Press

152nd YEAR   No. 61   THURSDAY, MARCH 2, 1972   Entered as Second Class Matter At Postoffice, Babylon and Bay Shore, N.Y.   5 CENTS

Firemen Save 2 Tots, Uncle Dies in Blaze

Two firemen, braving intense heat and smoke, rescued two little girls from a blazing Brooklyn apartment last night.

Responding to a 9:47 p.m. alarm at 119 Waverly Place, Fort Greene, Fireman George Kreusher, 32, assigned to Ladder Co. 102 and Fireman John Carney, 32, assigned to Rescue Co. 2, broke through the door of the third-floor apartment. Despite heavy smoke and heat, they found and rescued Kelly McKie, 3, and her year-old sister, Dawn.

The children, both unconscious, were huddled under a bed. Both are reported in critical condition at Cumberland Hospital. Also taken unconscious from the burning bedroom was the children's uncle, Ike Haskins, 45, who died later in the same hospital.

Long Island Press

Dramatic rescue in Bedford-Stuyvesant, Brooklyn.

Photo by Alex Donchin

Rescue Company 1, left to right: George Kreuscher, Bill Riley, Lt. Martin Cuniff, Hank Gonzalez.

Carrying a fallen brother.

George Kreuscher and Rescue Company 1's 1972 Mack Truck.

Kheel Tower.

Rescue 1's old back room, left to right: Dan Killoran, George Kreuscher, John Driscoll, Captain Brian O'Flaherty, Dennis Horrigan.

George Kreuscher–Rescue Company 1.

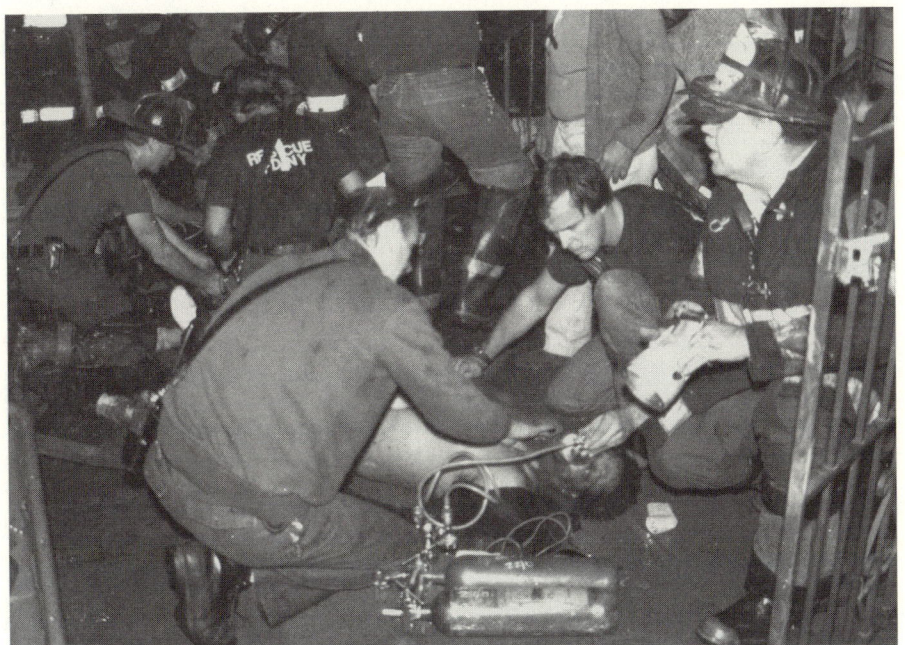

Rescue Company 1 administering to fire victims, left to right: George Kreuscher, Dan Killoran, Barry Meade.

Rescue Company 1 standing fast, left to right: Dick Martinsen, Pere Olsen (visiting fireman from Sweden), Lt. Frank Miali, Jimmy Rogers, Bill Riley, Chris Gliana, George Kreuscher.

Photo by Heldur J. Netolny

George Kreuscher inside Rescue Rig.

President Ronald Reagan greets each fireman standing by at a heliport in Manhattan, left to right: George Kreuscher, Eddie Wysocki, Barry Meade. Bill Riley is behind Lt. Moran and members of Engine 34.

Rescue 1 and other members digging the live victim out of a collapsed building.

Rescue 1 diver George Kreuscher directing hoseline under a pier, Washburn Wire Works at East River and 118th Street, Manhattan.

Photo by John Pedin

Rescue Company 1, south of the aircraft carrier "Intrepid," left to right: George Kreuscher, Jack Theobald, Mike McLaughlin (Ladder Company 4), John Driscoll, Lt. John Cerato, Capt. Brian O'Flaherty, Paul Hashagen.

Photo by Robert Athanas

Leif Kreuscher of Ladder Company 102.

Photo by Laura Yanes

Front—1948 Mack Rescue Spare. Rear—Rescue 1's 1972 Mack Rescue Rig.

Rescue 1 diver George Kreuscher in dry suit.

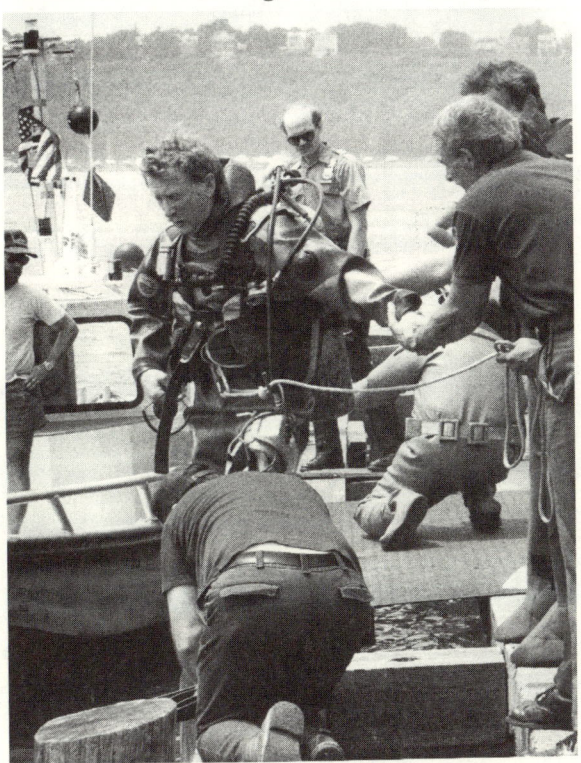

Photo by Tom Monaster, New York Daily News

Rescue 1 diver Jack Boyle in wet suit.

Center—Instructor Walter Hendrick of Lifeguard Systems with rescue divers. Left—George Kreuscher. Right—Paddy Brown.

Rescue 1 stands by as George Kreuscher peruses "GQ" magazine, left to right: Dave Williams, John Driscoll, Dan Killoran, Lt. Jay Fischler.

Photo by Paul Hashagen

Rescue 1, early morning in Harlem, left to right: Dave Williams, Dan Killoran, George Kreuscher, Captain Brian O'Flaherty, Tom Reichel with Joe Angelini above.

Sons Brandt and Leif with George Kreuscher.

The Rescue 1 study group for Lieutenant, left to right: Front, John McAllister, George Kreuscher. Rear, Al Fuentes, Bill Bessman, Barry Meade.

Photo by Mary Meade

Bill Bessman's promotion day, left to right: Bill Bessman, Al Fuentes, Paddy Brown, George Kreuscher, Margaret Bessman, and John McAllister with back to camera.

Promotion day, left to right: Maria and son George, George and Mary Lou Kreuscher, daughter Erika, son Leif, and Debbie.

Lookalikes. Left Captain Jack Caulkin of Ladder 43 and Lieutenant George Kreuscher.

Photo by D. Mochary

Tweed Gallery, New York City Hall. Exhibit of art work of artist Jesse Gardner, left to right: George Kreuscher with sons Leif and George. The portraits are of "Lt. Kreuscher" and "Wounded Fireman," son George Kreuscher.

Waldbaum's fire-front cover of the *Daily News*.

Courtesy of the New York Daily News

Waldbaums's fire-centerfold of the *Daily News*.

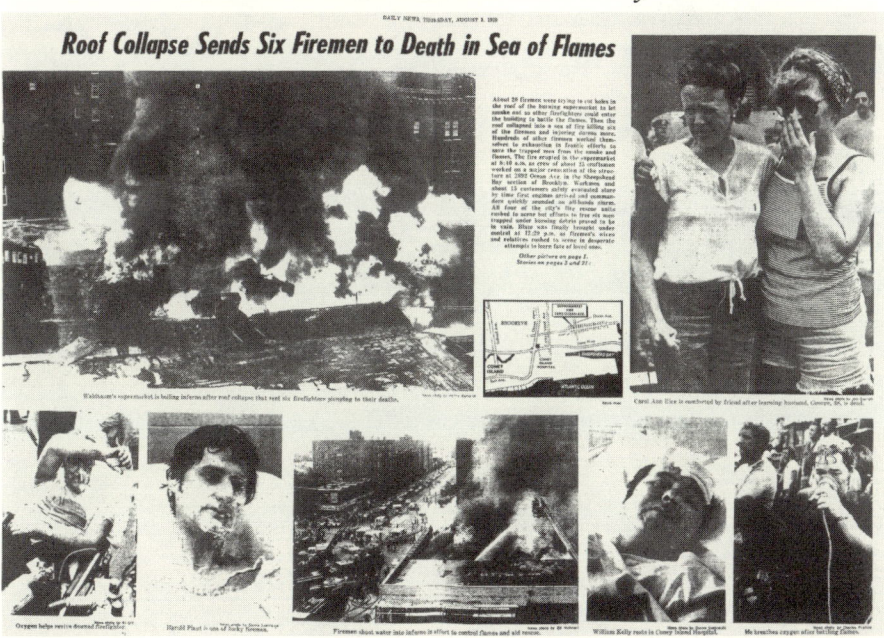

Courtesy of the New York Daily News

Ladies on the roof—centerfold of the *Daily News*.

Courtesy of the New York Daily News

Dan Killoran and Bob Burns assist diver George Kreuscher.

Photo by Tom Monaster, Courtesy of the New York Daily News

CHAPTER 15

Ring Jobs and the Ring Job

Since the inception of the Rescue Company, it has always been assumed they would solve any unusual occurrence or problem that came their way. It is still this way to this day.

The company's first notable job was a dangerous submarine fire at the Brooklyn Navy Yard in 1918.

In 1970, Rescue 1 rescued a man who had been impaled on one-inch-square pickets through his stomach, lungs, pelvis, and buttocks. A whole section of the steel fence with the pickets was cut off with oxyacetylene torches and the man was transferred to St. Vincent's Hospital with the pickets still in him. Rescue 1 was later special-called back to St. Vincent's to scrub up and don sterile clothing to assist surgeons in prying out one of the pickets, which was embedded in the man's pelvis.

Through the last 90 years, FDNY Rescue Companies have encountered many instances like these at one time or another. Although these are big, complex, and challenging jobs, there are many more smaller and less complicated jobs that are also highly unusual.

In our first aid kit, we carried things that we might need at a moment's notice, including a small device with a one-inch carbide-toothed wheel for cutting rings off swollen fingers. Of course, it's called the "ring cutter." It's a handy tool for cutting things made of soft metals like gold, silver, or brass, provided they are not too big. However, other metals, such as stainless steel, are so hard that the ring cutter won't even score them. So there are times when the "ring cutter" is useless.

One Sunday morning, Rescue 1 is special-called to St. Vincent's Hospital on Twelfth Street. We are told that the call is to remove a ring that police emergency has broken two ring cutters on. If the material of the ring is too hard, the thin, hard carbide-toothed wheel will break, as it has in this case. At this time, the only other removal method I know of is to cutting it off with a cold chisel and hammer.

When we get there, I see that this is a huge man with big fingers. The finger with the ring is twice the size of a big toe. The ring is thick and made of an extremely hard metal. I suggest taking him down to the cellar maintenance area to find something to use as an anvil to hold the ring on in order to split it open with a hammer and cold chisel. The chisel cracks the ring in two pieces, the man raises his ring finger hand in exclamation, then bolts out without as much as a word of thanks.

Another special call to remove a ring was for the head surgeon at Mt. Sinai Hospital. After holding his hand in ice-cold water for quite some time, the swelling had not gone down enough to remove the ring. It was a large college ring that the "ring cutter" could not cut. Lieutenant John Cerato had ground down a tablespoon so that it could be slipped under the ring to protect the surgeon's flesh while we cut down on the ring with the pneumatic 20,000-rpm Whizzer carborundum wheel. This tool is used in muffler shops to cut the bolts off old exhaust systems on cars.

We cut the ring in two places and it was removed, but the beautiful gold "Notre Dame" ring was partially destroyed.

The next day, when I tell my brother Ray what we had done, he tells me, "You could have gotten it off with a string." He is an operating engineer, a land surveyor in heavy construction. Being a good mechanic, once told how to do this, he would remember it.

The way it works is to take about six feet of strong, thin string, like Dacron fishing line, and squeeze a couple of inches of the line under the ring toward the body, at the fleshy part of the underside of the swollen ring finger. Then, keeping the finger straight, tightly wind the long length of the string toward the distal end of the finger, away from the body, with each coil touching the other, over the knuckle. Then, unwind the short end of the string, from the body side toward the finger tip, making sure the finger stays straight so as to prevent breaks between the coils. Unravel toward the tip of the finger and the ring slowly slides over the knuckle. Done right, it never fails.

Every attempt we ever made with the string, which was about a dozen times, we were successful. But no matter how good or effective a tool or method is, it does not always apply to every situation.

Late one afternoon in 1990, a short time before I got promoted out of Rescue 1, the department phone rings. Jackie Boyle picks it up, hangs up, and says, "It's the Manhattan dispatcher; they're special-calling us to St. Vincent's Hospital." This is the same hospital that so many special calls have come from over the years. Then Jackie says, "It's a ring job, and they'll give us the particulars when we get there." We respond to Greenwich Village.

As we get to the emergency room entrance, there are already other fire companies and hospital staff people there, awaiting our arrival. We have had time to think about this, discuss it, and decide what tools to bring in case we need them. This is Greenwich Village and we know that there are a multitude of possibilities, but we can't imagine what we are getting into.

The firefighters who are already there, among them 5 Truck, the Greenwich Village ladder company, all have big Cheshire Cat smiles on their faces. There are many nurses and a couple of doctors to escort us in, and the whole entourage of fast-walking doctors and nurses in their surgical dress take us in tow through the long hallways. We are carrying various tools and extra air bottles to be used to power the pneumatic tools we are carrying. It is a long walk, the length of the hospital, so as we hustle along, we are speculating with the usual "fireman banter," which is much like jailhouse humor. We reach our destination and the whole group stops before this furthest room—Room 108.

Now everyone becomes silent as a neat young doctor puts his hand on the closed door and gives us a look that indicates the seriousness of this situation. He holds the palm of his hand on the door as he raises one eyebrow, and simply says, "There's not one ring, but three of them." The doctor opens the door and we, Rescue 1, all go in, following Lieutenant Kenny Memnan.

Our group includes Lieutenant Ken Memnan, Jackie Boyle (my good friend from our 102 Truck days), Tommy Baker, Harvey Harrell, and me. We are just inside the room now that is pretty empty, except for a gurney across the room in the corner. There is a man lying on it who's completely covered by a draped sheet. All I can see are his eyes, which are looking at us in an almost desperate way. Covered as he is, there is no telling what we're dealing with, but we're sure it's serious.

Jackie Boyle, former paratrooper and boxer, an aggressive, straightforward man, crosses the room to the gurney, grabs a corner of the sheet, and says, "Let's see what we've got here." My brain cannot immediately catch up to what my eyes are seeing. The naked man lying there supine has the largest genitalia I have ever seen in my life. His scrotum is so enlarged that his testicles are the size of "Nerf" foam footballs. The penis is about a foot long and two inches thick. Three stainless steel rings are at the base of the testicles and the penis, up against his pubis, squeezing everything forward down to their one-and-a-quarter-inch inside diameter. If the testicles and penis were not swollen, it would still be a wonder how he got the penis and testicles through those rings. Despite how swollen his genitalia is, it's still hard to comprehend, almost unreal.

The man is past the point of embarrassment and just watches as we decide what to do. We decide to use the pneumatic Whizzer tool with the three-inch carborundum abrasive wheel. The problem, however, is that his flesh is swollen around the rings, making it impossible to cut the rings without cutting and injuring him more.

We decide to use the spoon that Captain John Cerato had ground down to fit under the rings. This will protect and press the skin away from the area being cut. The rings are pressed so tightly against the man's pubic bone by the engorged, swollen flesh of the testicles and penis that they must all be cut together, because we can't separate them to cut them individually.

Harvey Harrell slips the spoon under the rings to pull them out of the flesh while protecting it from the 20,000-rpm abrasive cutting wheel. I am the one who is doing the cutting, and I know that to cut stainless, I have to place the cutting blade on the rings at maximum rpm. I give it a try and the rings get hot almost instantly. The man recoils reflexively. There has been such perfusion into his genitals that he is as sensitive as is if he had an infection in this area. Lieutenant Memnan gets water bags from the staff and plays water on the rings while I cut with the Whizzer. The staff keep bringing replacement bags of isotonic water as the lieutenant empties each one on the cut. It takes a couple of minutes and we are through all three rings.

A second cut is necessary because each ring is about five-sixteenths of an inch thick, making them tough and impossible to open at the kerf (cut). Harvey proceeds to try to turn the rings, so the kerf will be facing down, enabling us to cut the opposite side of all three rings. The man recoils again and speaks the first words he has said to us: "I'll turn them. I know my own pain tolerance." The engorged flesh was pushing into the opening of the cut, so we let him do it. He turns the rings and Harvey replaces the spoon under them. Kenny Memnan keeps water on the rings and I continue to cut. In another couple of minutes, we are through all three rings again and this time, they just fall away.

It is hard to imagine this man's relief after having these rings removed. He instantly and feverishly begins rubbing the area where the rings have been. It looks to us like he will be facing an ordeal as a result of this loss of circulation and engorgement for so long.

When Lieutenant Memnan was using the water, a bag would last about 30 seconds, and we were cutting for six or seven minutes, flooding the floor.

The doctor who brought us in takes possession of the six ring halves. He tells us the patient has had these rings on for two days, trying to bring the swelling down with ice. It didn't work, so he had to come to the hospital wearing nothing but a dressing gown, because he couldn't wear pants or underwear.

Later, of course, there was some good-natured kidding about this whole incident. But from the time we entered that room and saw this person's dire situation, we treated it as the serious business it was.

None of us had ever seen rings like these before; apparently, they are used for sails on sailboats. As for how this man got all his parts through a ring with an inside diameter of one-and-one-quarter inches, that is pure speculation, but it could only have been done one part at a time.

Two nights later, when I returned to work for a night tour, there were roses on the kitchen table with an invitation to dinner from the victim. This was a sham set up by the men.

When Lieutenant Memnan filed his report on the incident with the accompanying diagram, it was thought that it was a joke. It wasn't. However, copies of that report found their way into surrounding city fire departments.

Postscript:
Harvey Harrell, an eager, enthusiastic, and cheerful firefighter, would be killed at the World Trade Center on September 11, 2001, as a lieutenant of Rescue Company 5, along with his whole crew.

CHAPTER 16

School Fire at Fifty-First Street and First Avenue

Davey Williams and I are the rescue above fire team, as we climb the already extended aerial to the roof. The ladder is at equilibrium, barely touching the roofline, with the tip six feet above.

I'm in front of Davey, carrying the saw and a hand tool as I mount the roof, sliding around the top of the ladder, with one foot on the roof and one foot still on the ladder. I say something to Dave that's rarely said, simply because it is often obvious enough. With grave emphasis, looking first at the roof and then back to Davey, I say, "Davey, this is highly dangerous." I know he already knows it, but I say it for emphasis.

Heavy black and brown smoke is pushing out of everywhere and it's clear there is a lot of fire under us; there are already truckmen on this dangerous roof, attempting to open it up.

This is a large, old school building that is four 15-foot stories high. The danger I see here as we mount the roof is that there is a trussed rain roof that is another story higher. It is made of plywood, covered with tar paper and tar. These are the same conditions that killed six firemen 10 years before at Waldbaum's Supermarket in Brooklyn.

One of the truck companies is already cutting a hole at the highest point, in the middle of this humpbacked, bowed rain roof. They are in a very dangerous spot with smoke engulfing them as they cut.

It makes no sense for Davey and me to be adding to the weight up there, so we go to the raised corner of the roof and proceed to cut.

The smoke is pushing out under pressure through the cuts, with fire behind it. Our situation up here is so perilous that I can only chance a small three-foot by three-foot hole. As I complete the last cut for the square, the sheathing is sucked in and a violent 30-foot tongue of fire shoots up and out of the hole. It drives Davey and me back. We now know the cockloft between the top floor and roof is fully involved in fire. This truss roof will not stand up to this volume of fire for very long.

The ladder company completes their hole with the same conditions as ours. The officer of the truck tells me to keep an eye on these young guys while he tries to see what is underneath us. It is getting really bad up here.

The truck officer returns and says, "We've got to get off this roof." There is a bulkhead stairway at the back of the 100-foot by 100-foot building.

There is so much fire coming out of the holes we have cut toward the front and middle that we all work our way along the treacherous catwalk with no parapet or railing, alongside the rain roof, at least 60 feet above the street.

When we get to the back, the smoke coming out of the bulkhead is awful. There are quite a few men back there, all balking at going down these stairs into God knows what. It seems this is the only way down. The officers are busy coaxing some of the young firemen down. I'm the last in a line of around 10 guys, who all have Scott Air Pak masks that might help them get past the fire.

We almost always have masks with us, but because I was carrying the saw up the aerial to a roof operation, I left my mask behind. All these guys with masks are having a hard time getting down and I'm beginning to think that I had better look for another way.

The only other way I know of is the aerial ladder, at the front of the building. To get to it, I'd have to go back along the catwalk, along the side of the truss roof and then go up and over the truss, between two holes of massive fire. It's not a great situation, but I am desperate.

As I am heading forward on the catwalk, getting the courage to go over the top of the truss roof, I hear Captain Brian O'Flaherty's voice saying, "Where are you going?" I look to the sound ahead of me and I see his head in a small pillbox structure I had not noticed earlier, slightly above the level of the roof. Without hesitation, pointing to him, I say, "There!" The roof is so bad that I dive head first, through the small window opening and unceremoniously climb down the six foot, three inch body of the rescue captain.

He says, "I thought you were going to get the saw." I say, "I forgot about that saw a long time ago."

As it turned out, all the fire was in that rain roof and it didn't take too much longer to get it under control.

An interesting sidelight to this fire is that it was the site of the Beekman Mansion, where General William Howe of the British Army had his headquarters after the Battle of Brooklyn during the Revolutionary War. This would eventually become Fifty-First Street and First Avenue.

When Nathan Hale was captured, he was interrogated and detained on this spot. This occurred the night before he was hung as a spy at Forty-Fourth Street and Vanderbilt Avenue, which is near Grand Central Terminal today.

CHAPTER 17

Funerals and Memorials

On August 27, 2006, a Sunday, we are at the wake for Tommy Baker, a longtime member of Rescue 1 and formerly of Ladder 108 in Brooklyn and Ladder 44 in the Bronx. Tommy was an excellent fireman and a popular guy. The place is packed with old friends and family. There are many uniforms from the active and also retired men who worked with him.

A fireman's wake is much in the Irish tradition. The deceased kept the faith, led a good life, loved his family, and was a credit to his profession. There is a somberness in the loss of a respected and loved person. On the other hand, they are often noisy affairs in the celebration of a life well spent. Sometimes, they are for older men who have had full lives, active and retired. There are times they are for young men who have died in the line of duty, with their whole life before them. There is everything in between with the same sadness for loss and celebration of that life.

Tommy Baker was 55 years old when he died after heart surgery, leaving his wife, Lorraine, and their three young adult children, a daughter and two sons.

At Tommy's wake, word passes that five firemen are missing at a fire in the Bronx. This puts another edge on an already somber day. Before we leave, we find out that the men have been found in the one-story building, where they had fallen into the cellar of a collapsed floor. It is still grave news. One of the firemen is dead, one is extremely critical, and three others are hospitalized.

The dead fireman is a 25-year-old former Marine who had been in Iraq with four months on the FDNY. He is Michael Reilly of Engine 75. The extremely critically wounded man is Lieutenant Howard Carpluk of Engine 42, who will die the next day, after heroic efforts by the doctors to save his life.

It is now a few days later and I go to East Islip for the funeral of Lieutenant Howard Carpluk, who leaves a wife and a young son and daughter. It is raining, and it will rain all day. Michael Reilly's funeral was yesterday in Ramsey, New Jersey.

On another beautiful afternoon, on Montauk Highway in East Islip, I am at one of the many memorials being held at the time. We are in front of Saint Mary's Roman Catholic Church for the memorial for a young fireman, Thomas Kennedy of Ladder 101, Brooklyn.

It is October 24, 2001, and there have been so many funerals and memorials that our ranks are getting thin. Hundreds of firemen are here, but it is still not the attendance this sacrifice deserves. There have been six weeks of these memorials in the five counties of New York City and the seven surrounding counties, plus New Jersey and Connecticut.

We are standing in the street in front of the church in ranks, waiting for the memorial for Fireman Kennedy, when two buses pull in nearby and unload. They are filled with 100 firemen from Los Angeles, California, in uniform. They form up and march toward us. They are big, robust-looking men with great tans. They are a handsome-looking group. As they come by, we all applaud them as they fill our ranks. This happens often, but this afternoon it is especially appreciated by everyone here. They are needed.

A fireman's funeral is an impressive thing to see. Firemen from as far away as Texas and California and Canada will come to New York for a fireman who died in the line of duty. There is a sea of blue uniforms along an avenue or street as far as a person can see. Thousands attended the funeral of Michael Reilly of Engine 75. The funeral of Lieutenant Carpluk of Engine 42 is the same. I am there, as well as my sons, Leif and George. We never see each other, which is often the case.

On September 11, 2001, the attack on the World Trade Center killed 343 firefighters and officers of the FDNY. Given that most fire departments, except for the biggest cities, don't have that many firefighters, it is a number that is hard to comprehend,.

When we came back from California, Mary Lou and I knew we were coming back to many funerals, which would also include memorials for unrecovered victims. Two-thirds of the firefighters as well as the civilians remained unrecovered. There were no bodies. Among the unrecovered was Joe Romagnolo, the husband of our goddaughter, Sandy. Joe left Sandy with their four children, who ranged in age from 10 down to infancy. Coincidentally, the genders and ages of their children are spaced exactly as our three boys and a girl. Joe was on the 105th Floor of the North Tower, maintaining communications for Cantor-Fitzgerald, when the first plane hit.

The foldouts with the pictures of the dead firefighters and officers resemble high school yearbooks. The number probably exceeds most high schools.

Mary Lou accompanied me to the wakes and funerals of those we had both known. There were others that only I knew. There were also firefighters or officers from companies I had been in, but who I never knew personally.

In the following months, I would get up in the morning and check the FDNY website to see the lineup of the funerals or memorials being held that day. I'd then pick and choose the ones I would attend. The priorities were a personal friend, the son of a friend, and a member of a company I had been a member of, or any memorial or funeral I was free to make that day. The only company I had been a member of where the men weren't all killed was Leif's company, Ladder 102. These were all serious, line-of-duty deaths as well as our first war dead of the war on terror that has resulted from this evil attack on America.

Leif, George, and I were at memorials and funerals most days and rarely were together at the same ones. It was impossible to make them all. There were a couple of Saturdays when there were 20 funerals or memorials on one day. We would run from one to the other and maybe make three of them in a day.

I was asked to eulogize Joe Angelini of Rescue 1, who had just celebrated 40 years with the FDNY. This is a great feat for a fireman. I was honored to be able to do it. Joe and his son Joe Jr. of Ladder 4 were both killed that day. However, Mary Lou and I had to leave Joe's funeral after the eulogy, before the service ended, in order to attend the funeral of another very good friend, Battalion Chief Dennis Cross, which was held within an hour of Joe's.

There were days when I knew more of the firemen whose memorials and funerals were taking place than I could attend. The last of these was the memorial for Gary Geidel of Rescue 1, on August 21, 2002, almost one year later. I had gone to High Angle Rescue School with Gary and knew him well. He had been an Eagle Scout and a Marine. His father, Paul, was my lieutenant in Rescue 1 and I had known Gary's brother, Mike, for all his years in the FDNY. Mike is also a member of Rescue 1. Mike survived only because he wasn't working that day. Memorials are very strange in that there are only pictures and memories.

The FDNY Emerald Society Pipes & Drums numbers about 50 men and is a highly rated band. They are bagpipers and drummers who play at all FDNY celebrations of joy and sadness. They were stretched so thin that there were sometimes just a few members or only one available to play at some of the funerals and memorials. Sometimes, volunteers from other fire departments and civilian bands would augment their ranks. It was all heart-rending, reaching-out sadness, shared by all.

One night, I am sitting in a busy pizza parlor, waiting for a couple of takeout pies. Chris Corbin, another fire officer of the FDNY, comes in. We are glad to see each other. Chris has been playing bagpipes to the point of exhaustion, like all the rest of the bagpipers. He tells me how he thought he was getting sick, but luckily it was just the pace of the last year. We had gone to FDNY officers' school together. He is a former Marine. We share some small talk for a while until my pizza is ready. We both stand to bid each other goodbye and when we look at each other it is so emotional, we hug each other in the middle of this busy pizza place. I have a slight hint of tears in my eyes as we part. That's just the way it is with us firemen.

CHAPTER 18

Things That Happen on Any Day

The Stamp Machine

The woman is standing on a small platform, supported by a couple of firemen. She is an older office worker who has just caught her finger in a $10,000 stamp machine. She has been here a while and, besides being embarrassed, she is somewhat distressed.

Apparently, a stamp didn't come down from the machine, which is used every day in the office. Unthinkingly, the woman put her finger up into the opening to retrieve the stamp, and her finger got caught in the cutter that would have normally separated the stamp from the roll inside the machine. The sharp, knife edge of the cutter, which is holding her finger, is angled away from her, so she is caught like in one of those Chinese finger puzzles that will not release the finger when the person tries to pull it out.

Now, there is a big group of firemen all around her, with all their turnout gear. They've made many attempts to get her finger out without cutting her badly, but her finger is tightly caught. The captain, Brian O'Flaherty, decides we should dismantle the expensive machine.

First, we take off the outer cowling, only to find out the machine is more complicated than we could have imagined. We have the Whizzer with its 20,000-rpm, three-inch carborundum disc. The captain tells Jimmy Emery to start cutting away pieces of the machine, in order to get closer to the lady's finger. The closer we get, the more distressed the woman becomes.

Firemen are switching off with one another, supporting the woman, who cannot sit down because the floor is too far down from where her finger is stuck. Fellow office workers are bringing cold compresses for her head and neck to keep her from fainting.

Jimmy cuts one piece after the other; this is taking time, so I relieve him and start to get very close to her finger. We have literally destroyed this machine, removing it piece by piece down to her finger. She is perspiring profusely and almost faints from this ordeal. I am cutting at 20,000 rpms within an inch of her finger and that, combined with the high-pitched sound of the tool, is making her very nervous. I am steady and very close to her finger. I know we will get her free.

In her excitement about the tool being so close to making the final cut, she involuntarily moves her finger in and out, extricating herself.

Cutting Myself Off

One night up in Harlem, there is a multiple alarm fire for a six-story tenement. The top couple of floors are burning merrily and the fire has gotten into the cockloft.

When we get there, the chief puts us to work. These are row tenements of brick and steel with brick firewalls between buildings that prevent fire from spreading from building to building in most cases. There are 50-foot-deep open air shafts that open at the rear between each building. The front halves of the buildings are separated by a brick wall that forms a three-foot-high parapet above the front 50-foot depth of the building.

Davey Williams and I trudge up the stairs of the so-far safe adjacent building. I am carrying the Partner circular saw with carbide tip blades to help open the roof of the fire building. We can hear the sound of saws going on the front of the roof; it seems most of the fire is in the cockloft. The truckmen are still busy trying to open up everything they can.

There is enough fire for everyone, with a lot of activity on the roof toward the front. So Davey and I step over the parapet at the front half of the building and work toward the rear of the fire building, which has open shafts on both sides.

Heavy black smoke is pushing out of the cornice at the front of the fire building, with a couple of floors of fire beneath us. There is so much smoke and fire that we feel free to start cutting a big five-foot by five-foot hole over one of the rear apartments. The trucks are just about finishing the same function in the front, where the smoke has gotten worse.

I make the necessary cuts on all four sides, finishing on the windward side. I cut out a corner of the square so Davey can get a purchase, and he pulls up the tarred tin and sheathing in one piece. Davey's a big man and he does this more easily than most. It is never easy. The smoke and heat belch out of there and we feel it is so productive that we will make another five-foot by five-foot hole above the apartment next door.

We can tell by the extremely dry heat and smoke that the cockloft space below us and the top floor is fully involved, even though we haven't seen fire yet back where we are. We repeat the roof cuts on the other side. Davey pulls the sheathing up and the whole roof is now engulfed in thick, acrid smoke. As he pulls the sheathing, he's toward the front, while I am to the rear of the two holes we have cut and opened. Turning to retrieve the saw, I see fire is lapping above the roof, out of the rear windows, eliminating the fire escape as a way off the roof.

In seconds, Davey has stepped away from the hole toward the front, to get out of that terrible heat and smoke. This is instinctive behavior for an experienced fireman. However, by being on the rear side of the holes, with open shafts on both sides, I have momentarily trapped myself. I have to get to the front, where Davey stepped moments before.

The only way for me to go is up the middle on my hands and knees, between the two big holes that have disappeared in all the heavy smoke.

Crawling on hands and knees when there is no visibility shifts a fireman's center of gravity further back, possibly preventing him from falling into a hole he would surely go into when walking.

It is so bad up here that, even though I know the direction to the front, I have to make a blind judgment as I crawl between these two very productive holes we have cut.

Crawling blindly into the dense smoke, I push the saw in front of me, pushing it on its blade. I figure I would rather see the saw fall into one of the holes before I do. It is not far to go, but the crawl forward is filled with trepidation.

As I get through, Davey is waiting for me and I relate what happened in these few seconds we were separated. We have a very short laugh, shake our heads, and get off the roof the way we came. A short while later, we stand by as the bulkhead in the center of the roof sinks into the blazing collapse.

The Lighted Canyon

It is late in the afternoon on a crystal clear day in February, the wind is blowing 50 mph, and it is freezing. Rescue 1 has been special-called to Twenty-Ninth Street and Seventh Avenue. This is one block down from what was once Tin Pan Alley, the heart of the music business of the early twentieth century, in the days of Ira and George Gershwin.

The report is that metal sheathing has blown off of the roof of a tall building, which is a danger to people in the street. The building is Kheel Tower, a 21-story building constructed in 1926.

The penthouse structure on top of this building has a hip-type roof with four sloping sides and is clad in light green, copper-plated steel sheathing. The sheathing has partially rotted away over the years and it is being blown loose and flapping in the strong winds today. The pieces are 20 feet long, sloping vertically, and interlocked and nailed to wood sleepers in the concrete structure. A 3-foot by 20-foot piece has already fallen into the street.

Despite the severe wind and cold, we take turns nailing the flapping sheathing down one piece at a time, using a portable ladder that's leaning against the penthouse, nailing at the bottom and as high as we can reach, which is about one-third of the way up.

The hip-style roof actually has a flat 6-foot by 20-foot platform on top instead of a ridge. It is surrounded by a 2-foot ornamental fence on all sides. Lieutenant Steve Casani and I check to see how we can get on top of this structure. There is a narrow porthole onto the roof of the penthouse, which I am able to get through fairly easily. Most of the men of the rescue company are big, powerful men who would have trouble getting through this porthole. With some effort, Steve Casani squeezes up through the porthole behind me.

The two of us now reach over the side, 267 feet above the ground, to tack the sheathing down as far down as we can reach. We are busy working and forget the cold and hardly realize that day has turned to night. We finish tying down all the loose metal sheathing and then stand up, sort of on top of the world in the middle of the lighted magnificence of midtown Manhattan.

We look around and there we are, 267 feet above the street, with the valley of lighted skyscrapers all around us. This is a rare view, where we can see in every direction almost at the same time—the Empire State Building to our north, the World Trade Center to our south, and every lighted building in between. We could never have imagined this never-to-be-forgotten bonus. We are surrounded by a "Grand Canyon of Light," standing on top of a building in the middle of Manhattan.

You Can't Make This Up

Because there is so much fire throughout this Lower East Side tenement and it's already a multiple alarm, all the members of Rescue 1 are together. At most fires, we are separated, sometimes singly, but most times in pairs, in different parts of a building or buildings.

This is a large apartment-type tenement with many floors and four apartments on each floor. There is a lot of fire on the upper floors and it's traveling downward through pipe traces and other vertical voids, spreading in the ceilings of apartments below. This is unusual, given that fire usually travels up.

Amazingly, there are still civilians on the lower floors who have not yet left the building. There are firemen all over the building, and the whole complement of the rescue company storms into one of the apartments directly below the fire. In our turnout gear with our tools, we take up a lot of room. The big men look even bigger as we fill the narrow hallway into the living quarters.

A male civilian has been caught in front of this stream of men, and he cannot get out. He apparently doesn't speak English and appears very agitated. We don't have time for him at the moment because we are chasing fire and we have to open parts of these ceilings to see if fire has dropped down here.

As we are pulling the ceilings with our six-foot hooks, the civilian looks very distressed at what we are doing. Of course, it is a mess of falling plaster, lath, and plaster dust.

Anton Vodvarka, former Army Special Forces, tall, powerful, and a proper gentleman, shows great deference toward the distressed and agitated civilian. He explains in great detail what we are doing and why. Anton lives in Greenwich Village and has a certain empathy for this person.

The civilian seems no less agitated as he nods to Anton, who has been talking to him loudly and descriptively in an attempt to get past the language barrier. The civilian is shaking his head, totally self-absorbed and distracted. He is trapped and evidently not happy with his situation. He will have to wait until we are done.

As it turns out, there is no fire down here. Now we can let the civilian by and free him from his short entrapment. As he goes into the public hallway, we can hear a crescendo of people screaming.

This little weasel of a man is a known local thief and he did not belong in the apartment. The civilians in the hallway sound as if they want to lynch this guy and he will be lucky if he gets arrested by the police to prevent it.

This thief was in the process of looting an apartment of a building that was on fire. He got trapped and caught by our presence in the apartment where he was operating.

The irony is that this man's distress, which we thought was the result of the damage we were causing to his apartment, was not that at all, but rather the uneasiness of a thief who has been caught.

CHAPTER 19

Elevators

Often, at fires in hotels, upper floors have to be checked for smoke conditions and people in distress. Elevators are often the easiest means to the many floors in large buildings, even though firefighters know full well that elevators can be problematic.

The fire department has procedures for when to use elevators under fire conditions and when not to. There are ways to use elevators in order to minimize risk, such as those elevators in blind shafts that pass the fire floor, enabling firefighters to get above the fire. If the elevator is in a shaft that opens to the fire floor, sometimes, out of necessity, these elevators are used and tested every five floors to make sure they can be stopped before the fire floor. Elevators with heat sensors that aren't in blind shafts can sometimes stop and open on the fire floor with dire consequences. In any case, under the best of circumstances, elevators always have the potential for danger and sometimes they cannot be used.

Elevators are the most common means of transportation from floor to floor in high-rise buildings. This often gives people using them a sense of complacency, even firefighters. However, they should never be taken for granted.

My very first emergency with Rescue 1 is to a special call to the Federal Courthouse at Foley Square in lower Manhattan, where Lafayette and Centre streets meet. The dispatch is for a person who fell in an elevator. That is all the information we have.

When we get there, I gather our first aid boxes and I am prepared to take care of injuries. The deputy chief tells us that the elevator fell to the basement and that is where we should go. Along the bank of elevator doors in the basement is the one open door with a couple of people standing outside. I have the first aid boxes, so, I go around them and step into the elevator looking at the floor. There is no one there.

I am just inside the elevator door and look to my left and there are two stockinged female legs hanging from the door retractors, up against the door. They are limp and lifeless. There are two emergency service cops on top of the elevator, working to move the whole elevator car back away from the door side to free the young woman. They move it enough so she can be slid free to us firemen. The poor thing is surely dead, with her head and chest crushed between the front wall of the shaft and the elevator car. We lower her gently to the floor. She is 29 years old, the same age as my wife, Mary Lou. It is a pitiful moment.

Screams rang out when the open elevator fell as people got off at the main floor. The screams came from witnesses as the top of the elevator doorway caught this poor girl at the back of her neck, like a guillotine, dragging her to the basement where we found her. I'm sure she was killed instantly. Imagine the end of a workday and the misfortune of being the last person to get off that elevator.

At this time, I've got about 10 years in the job and I'm new in the rescue company, without a lot of experience with elevators. Ladder 102 and Engine 230 were in Bedford-Stuyvesant, Brooklyn, where most of the elevators were in the public housing projects. Most times, at fires in these fireproof buildings, we used the stairs, avoiding the use of elevators. Once in a while, we removed someone who was stuck in one, but that was about it. Manhattan was different. All the high-rise buildings, hotels, and office buildings made general use of elevators, and consequently, so did the fire department.

We were often told of the dangers with elevators, but as a Brooklyn fireman, I didn't quite believe it. I personally took it with a grain of salt. In Manhattan, I learned quickly that the warnings were legitimate.

On August 3, 1977, Rescue 1 responded to an all-hands fire at the St. Martin Hotel. It is about 10:00 p.m. The fire is brought under control just as we arrive. Because hotels have a lot of people in them, the chiefs often use the rescue company to help with secondary searches on the floors above the fire in order to make sure there is no fire extension or people in distress. This is routine for us.

We all get in one of the two elevators at this old hotel. Lieutenant Tony Limberg intends to drop a couple of us off on every few floors in order to check out all the floors up to the top, which is the twelfth floor. This elevator is slow to respond and is somewhat erratic. It stops before each floor, then slowly gets even with the floor. The door opens slowly. We get out two by two, every couple of floors from the sixth to the twelfth.

The secondary searches and check of the upper floors are all negative, so Tony Limberg tells us to take up and pick him up at the top floor. As the elevator ascends, each of us gets on from whatever floor we are on. A very nervous woman resident is on the elevator; she had meant to be descending, but decided to stay on. We get on singly or in pairs going up. We take up a lot of room with our turnout gear and tools. For the most part, these are big men who look bigger than they are when decked out in fire clothing and Scott Air Paks.

Every time a guy gets on, this woman's eyes get bigger and bigger and she gets more nervous and flustered. At the twelfth floor, Tony Limberg gets on and the elevator is full as we descend.

I believe the woman is sorry she stayed on the elevator. She is standing next to the control panel near the door, facing sideways. I am standing right next to her. The others on the elevator are Lieutenant Tony Limberg, Philly Prial, who is the senior man, Joe Bryant, Danny Killoran, and Ernie Andreacci. The woman is very nervous, but I assure her that she is safe with the fire department.

Ernie is leaning against the back wall, next to Philly Prial, as we descend. We are relaxed and ready to get back to the firehouse. I no sooner tell the woman how safe she is than Philly yells and we suddenly hit the bottom like a ton of bricks. The elevator car is about a foot below the first floor and it has hit the bumper in the basement underneath. Tony Limberg instantly says, "Everybody stay as you are. Let's see what we've got here."

The woman is in a panic, her eyes are like saucers, but she doesn't move, spellbound. We have dropped six floors in a free-falling elevator car, with no sensation of falling. So much for the theory about jumping at the last second.

We have just regained our equilibrium when there's a tremendous impact on top of the elevator car. Years of dust comes down on us while we are still trying to figure out what has happened.

Until now, the woman has been quiet and motionless and looking straight ahead with those bulging eyes. The dust is still descending when she gives out a shrill scream: "Let me out of here." If she had any faith in us, I think she's lost it. She runs out screaming and we never see her again.

The second impact has really rocked us. As we assess the damage, we are well rattled, no different from people involved in an automobile accident. That impact and sudden stop are a trauma to a person's whole system.

Because Ernie had been leaning against the back, he broke his knee when we landed. Philly Prial was standing next to Ernie, looking at the diamond window on the door that allows people inside the car to know what floor they are on. Philly saw the sixth and lower floors flash past so fast that he just had time to yell and we were down in an instant.

The elevator hoist cable had broken when we were somewhere above the sixth floor, causing the car to fall. Apparently, the governors that should have stopped the car from free-falling failed to work. The second impact that hit the top of the car was a ton of steel hoist cable, which spun out of the hoist pulley a couple of seconds after we landed. The roof and frame of the car kept us from being crushed by the cable.

We hit with such force that we are all taken to St. Clare's Hospital for X-rays and observation. Philly Prial, a former U.S. Marine and survivor of the Chosin Reservoir in Korea, has a fracture of his spine and this will be his last tour with the FDNY. Ernie will be out for a year. The rest of us will be okay. Joe Bryant will become a battalion chief and a senior one at that.

Over the years, many people were simply trapped in elevators and we would have to get them out, sometimes simply by opening the doors with special tools and keys that we carried on the rig. At other times, it required locating the elevator car and if it was in a location where there was no door, we would breach the wall to get to the trapped people.

One night, we get special-called to one of the great New York hotels, for people caught in one of the elevators. The hotel personnel have been trying to find out where the elevator is. It turns out that they had been doing this for three and a half hours before we got there.

In short order, we are able to assess where the elevator is located with the help of a few reliable civilians. The hotel personnel were so intimidated by the owner of the hotel that they were trying to do this on their own without damaging the hotel, but at the expense of the poor people trapped in the elevator.

Once we get an idea where the elevator car is, we start listening from floors around the elevator shaft by making small holes in the walls. This makes the hotel personnel very nervous and they have to be removed from the area so we can do what we have to do.

Eventually, we find the exact location in a blind shaft and breach the masonry wall to get the people out. The elevator is full with about 15 people in it. Considering their four-hour ordeal, they are of remarkably good cheer, and very thankful and relieved that we have gotten them out.

There were times we got caught in elevators ourselves. However, we always had 10-pound steel hand tools, such as the Halligan tool, which is a multi-use lockbreaker tool. Busting out of an elevator would be a last resort, but in most cases we could do that.

This happens to Rescue 1 one night in another old hotel. We get into an elevator that appears okay. But once we are in and going up, the elevator stops at a floor, opens eight inches, then closes and goes on to the next floor. It eventually passes above the fire floor and continues to do the same thing, on floor after floor.

We hear on our radios that the chief is thinking of venting the smoke from the fire up through the elevator shaft we are in.

We are trying to keep radio silence about our predicament because of the understandable embarrassment of being Manhattan Rescue Company 1 and stuck in an elevator. So we remain silent, trying to keep the egg off our faces.

After going through the whole building like this, we find that a bolt is out of the door retractor, preventing the door from opening. Once we discover this, we are able to push the retractor arm with a tool and get out, our reputations intact. No one is the wiser and they never ventilate that way anyhow.

Whenever an elevator acts erratically or seems in any way unusual, get out at the first possible opportunity. When elevators fall, they fall suddenly, with such speed that there is no time to react.

If holding an elevator for someone, never use your body to prevent the door from closing; if the elevator drops suddenly, you will never be able to react to it in time.

Always use the stairs whenever possible, instead of the elevator, in all emergencies or fire situations.

Although there are a few wonderful stories of people who survived in elevators at the World Trade Center on September 11, 2001, we will never know how many people were trapped until the buildings came down and perished there.

CHAPTER 20

Honor

When the "Desert Storm" war ended, New York, as it always does, welcomes home the nation's warriors. It is an experience just to be there, to see those being honored marching up through the "Canyon of Heroes," which is lower Broadway and the financial district, with its impressive line of big buildings.

Because of the amount of paper that will shower down from these buildings, there is a fire watch at every block from the Battery up to City Hall Park at Park Row. There will be one fire officer along Broadway on every block, with firefighters standing by with extinguishers on every adjacent side street in the event of fire. This is more of a consideration now with the growing awareness of the possibility of terrorism taking place.

Lieutenants and captains will be posted in the middle of each block along the whole parade route. If they see a problem, they are to notify a firefighter standing on the side streets.

As the parade starts, there are flags waving and bands coming up Broadway on this beautiful sunny day. Then all the fighting units march along, resplendent in their combat uniforms. Each unit is led by guidons and battle flags with the names of all the great battles the unit has fought and victories it has won.

There are famous and not-so-famous U.S. Army combat infantry units, paratroopers in their red berets, and Special Forces in their green berets. Some of these are in dress uniforms with their pants tucked into the ever-present paratrooper combat boots. There are United States Marines coming by, crisp-looking as usual, and sailors and Navy Seals who have also fought in Desert Storm. Of course, there are Air Force personnel marching by representing the fighter and bomber pilots who fought the war, along with all their support personnel. They fill me with pride. I can't believe my good fortune in being here.

Behind the American units come segments of fighting units of our allies in Desert Storm. Among them are some British troops and some French troops. The French troops are represented by the distinctive, serious-looking French Foreign Legion, carrying their combat submachine guns held against their chests in parade formation, eyes straight ahead.

This goes on for hours. The printer paper comes down like snow, and we're wading through the paper on the ground. The din of the jubilant, welcoming crowds lining Broadway is so loud that almost nothing else can be heard above the tumultuous roar of joy and appreciation for the job well done.

A contingent from the Congressional Medal of Honor Recipients Society from past wars are among the Americans marching up this celebrated canyon. Many are very old and ride seated in two flatbed trucks with side rails. There are about 50 of these old and infirm warriors riding on these trucks. There are some old bulldog faces that signal the courage and toughness of these men.

About 100 Medal of Honor recipients who are either younger or healthy enough to walk march in front of the trucks. I am standing at my post in the roadway in front of the crowd. As they pass, I recognize one of the hundreds marching by. It is Joe Foss, looking like John Wayne. He was one of America's greatest fighter pilots.

As a Marine captain flying the Corsair, Joe Foss shot down 26 enemy planes in the South Pacific. For this, he received the Congressional Medal of Honor. He is now a general.

After World Ward II, Joe Foss was a two-term governor of South Dakota and the first commissioner of the American Football League. He also hosted "The American Sportsman" on television.

When I discover him opposite me, I cannot think of any of these things, but I am trying to think of something fast that will let him know that I know who he is. I yell as loud as I can, "Joe Foss, president of the N.R.A." He hears me over the din of the crowd and reaches back from the middle of these marching legends and grabs my hand, shaking it vigorously. His eyes are shining from my recognition of him. While shaking my hand, he is saying something to me that, unfortunately, I cannot hear over the crowd. It doesn't really matter much, as long as he knows I recognized him. It is an unexpected highlight of a wonderful day among all these heroes. Again, the FDNY takes me to where the action is.

Since the days of President Nixon, whenever the president comes to Manhattan, the last leg of the trip in and the first leg out are usually by U.S. Marine Helicopter. Whichever helipad the president may land at, it is always guarded with the usual police and Secret Service personnel. In addition, the nearest fire department engine and truck companies stand by at the helipad, in fire gear, at the ready. Rescue 1, being the only rescue company in Manhattan, is specially assigned.

It is a high honor to stand guard for our president when he comes to town. This is taken quite seriously and enthusiastically. We know that if anything unforeseen happens while landing or taking off, we would be the ones who would have the honor to get him. This is a welcome and well-received responsibility.

I personally stood by for Presidents Gerald Ford, Jimmy Carter, and Ronald Reagan. A common thread through them all, upon seeing them close up, is how fit-looking they are. It is an inspiring thing to see the leader of our country looking so fit and ready for that awesome responsibility.

Most times, when the president is brought to the helipad to leave, his limo stops right in front of us. At the very least, every president, after disembarking from the limo for the helicopter, will wave or nod toward us in acknowledgment of our presence, fifteen feet away. Sometimes they take the time to greet us individually, going down the line of firefighters standing by, shaking hands with each one of us.

One beautiful evening, March 13, 1981, Rescue 1 is at the helipad for the helicopter takeoff of President Ronald Reagan. This night, as the president's limo comes into the helipad with the convoy of Secret Service cars and the cars of the reporters and photographers, the limo goes right to the steps of the helicopter. The Secret Service seems anxious to get the president onto the helicopter 100 feet away from us.

They get the president to the top landing of the steps to the helicopter. The president stops and, counter to the plan they had for him, we can hear him say, "I want to say hello to the firemen." He turns and comes back down the steps and walks toward us with that great, confident, athletic gait he has. He is a handsome man. He walks down the line and greets each of us with a smile and handshake. This is a real man who makes me proud of him and proud to be an American.

Unfortunately for the president and the rest of us, shortly after this, President Reagan was shot and we would never be able to be this close to him again.

CHAPTER 21

Another Phone Call

Friday night, July 9, 1993, is a sweltering, humid night. After shopping in the evening, Mary Lou and I have a peaceful dinner on the backyard deck. Our four kids are all adults now and we are enjoying this evening alone with each other, with full knowledge that if we wanted to, we could just take off and go somewhere with no immediate obligations to anyone. We're having a wonderful late outdoor dinner with prospects of the whole weekend free ahead of us.

We finish dinner around 10:00 p.m. and Mary Lou goes to bed while I catch up on some late evening television. Sometime after 11:00 p.m., the phone rings and snaps me out of my doldrums in front of the TV. Mary Lou is asleep. It is Lieutenant Charlie Schmid, our son George's officer in Engine 93, Washington Heights, Manhattan.

A call from the firehouse this late at night is unusual and alarming. Charlie Schmid and I know each other well and I know him to be a gentleman. With professional courtesy, he identifies himself. My brain is racing, and he knows that I am aware of what such a late night phone call from the firehouse can mean. So, as quickly as he can, he tells me that George will be all right, but that he was burned and has been brought to the New York Firefighters Burn Center at New York Hospital. Charlie's calm phone manner and his message give me a relative degree of relief.

George asked Charlie to call me first so I could break this bad news to his wife, Maria. It is a lousy call to make. As soon as I hang up the phone, I wake Mary Lou and tell her the news we have just received. She has been sound asleep and is shocked awake by this.

My most immediate concern, after this, is my phone call to Maria. I tell her as carefully as I can what happened to George with the information that Charlie has given me.

A molotov cocktail had been thrown at Engine 93's rig as they were responding to a reported gas leak at 187th Street and Audubon Avenue. I assure her that he will be all right, but that he was burned and brought to the Burn Center. She takes this bad news well under the circumstances. She tells me her brother will bring her to our house so we can all go to New York Hospital together. It is a 50-mile drive to New York Medical Center on the East Side of Manhattan.

Our daughter, Erika, is home this night, so she already knows what we know. Our son Leif is at his future wife Debbie's house, so we call him to let him know. Our son Brandt is in California, so we will wait to tell him later, when we have more details.

Maria arrives and immediately we all take the long late night drive into the city, carrying the anxiety of George's situation with us. Traffic is light and we're thankful for this small favor.

It is early morning and still dark when we drive up into the cobblestone courtyard of the old section of New York Hospital. There are a couple of official fire department cars still parked in the court. The deputy chief and his driver are in one of the cars. The chief, who I have known for a long time, is John McCormack. He covered as a young lieutenant in Rescue 1 when I was there. Both of them get out and offer their sympathies and try to fill us in on a few more of the details of what has happened. Chief McCormack was the chief who responded to the original emergency at which it all happened. Then his driver, with every consideration, escorts our family into the emergency room. We are Maria, Mary Lou, our daughter Erika, and our son Leif, who as far as I know, hasn't given a thought yet to being a fireman himself.

As we enter the emergency room at this late hour, it is still filled with fire department administration and union representatives of the Uniformed Firefighters Association. Chief McCormack's aide informs us that Mayor Dinkins has already been here, as well as the police commissioner, Ray Kelly. They are gone now, but all the fire department officials are still here. The room is busy with doctors and nurses tending to the wounded firemen.

We head right to a curtained-off cubicle where George is on a gurney, lying on his back, his burned arms and hands outstretched at his sides. He is a pitiful sight. This is a tough thing for loved ones to see, especially his wife and mother. Upon seeing him, we all take a turn kissing him, starting with Maria. I kiss him on his upper forehead, the only place I can see where he is not burned. He is badly wounded with burns to his face, hands, arms, and upper torso. What I notice right away is that his burned arms are stretched out away from him, holding his hands up, as the body fluids are dripping from the tips of his fingers onto the floor.

In the next bed, in a similar cubicle, is another fireman. He is Tommy Brannigan of Engine 67 and a classmate of George's from the Fire Academy. Coincidentally, they are good friends who were together tonight, because Tommy had been detailed to Engine 93 for this tour. Tommy is still and appears to be asleep. They have both been given morphine. He is a bookend to George. Still dirty and sooty, with the same burns, he is as pathetic-looking as George is, except that he doesn't appear to be awake.

Erika is not too easy at seeing her older brother in this state. So Mary Lou takes her out to the sitting area for a break. Ironically, this ordeal will drastically change Erika's life. She will leave Long Island Tourism to go back to school at Molloy College of Nursing. She eventually will become a Coronary Care Unit Nurse at Stony Brook University Hospital.

As Erika and Mary Lou enter the sitting area, they are approached by the 1st Deputy Fire Commissioner and former Assistant

Chief Bill Feehan. This man, who has seen it all, emits a warmth toward my wife and daughter that they will never forget. He comforts them and tells them that if there is anything he can do for them, they have only to ask. He is a man of his word.

On a St. Patrick's Day back in the mid-1980s, we have a clothing store on Madison Avenue that has a heavy smoke condition on the whole first floor with no fire or heat. So, Rescue 1 and the trucks are in the cellar trying to find the fire. Michael Killoran (a former wrestler and the nephew of Danny Killoran) and I are kneeling at a doorway to a room where the smoke is heavy and we think we hear fire crackling in the ceiling below the first floor. I turn to my side and kneeling right next to us is this handsome, slim, assistant chief in his "Class A" St. Patrick's Day dress uniform. He asks us if we think the fire is up there. He has heard our names being used back and forth and refers to us by name. The fire is there and that is my first exposure to Chief Feehan.

I would encounter Chief Feehan as an instructor of probationary firefighters and Special Projects collapse and other rescue training. He would often address the graduating probationary class and their families with the most eloquent and beautiful speeches, delivered without notes. Any instructor who was free would go to the mezzanine of the auditorium to see and hear something wonderfully inspiring and phenomenal. Chief Feehan would end every speech with the same Irish blessing:

> "May the road rise to meet you,
> May the wind be ever at your back
> May the sun shine warm upon your face
> And the rain fall softly on your fields
> And until we meet again,
> May God hold you in the hollow of his hand."

This remarkable and warm man, along with Chief of Department Pete Ganci, will die on September 11, 2001, at the World Trade Center, years past his retirement age.

Also in the emergency room is Mike Carter, who is vice president of the Uniformed Firefighters Association. He is a good guy and he also extends himself to us. He assures us that if we have to stay nearby, the union will take care of it and they do.

After I had made the phone calls to George's wife, Maria, and Leif, I also called Lieutenant Jimmy Curran, my good friend and partner in Special Projects at the Fire Academy on Randalls Island. Besides his calming effect, he is very helpful as to the procedures that will follow and what we should expect—a valuable friend.

I am standing with Maria and George for a while and start to get a better picture of what has happened this night. He tells me how the attack on them occurred. As a fireman myself, I want to know all the details.

Responding to a gas leak emergency, Engine 93, followed by 45 Truck, turns into 187th Street from Audubon Avenue, when a molotov cocktail is thrown through the window of the back of the cab, passing Timmy O'Connor, the new man. It goes across and over the engine compartment to the side where George and Tommy are sitting facing each other. In the enclosed compartment, they are not in their turnout coats. It is an extremely hot night.

The compartment on their side is instantly a ball of fire from their waists up. In the second it takes to come across, George sees the molotov cocktail come across in slow motion and then burst into a ball of fire, engulfing him and Tommy.

George is riding backwards, as a courtesy, to let Tommy ride face forward, as he is a detail from another company. This puts Tommy at the door and door handle. I ask George, "How long did it take you to get out? A second?" He thinks and through his discomfort he says, "Maybe two."

While in the ball of fire, George knows they are seconds from imminent death. Tommy is smart, strong, and a tough guy, so George is expecting the door to open immediately. He can see both his and

Tommy's legs beneath the ball of fire that's surrounding their heads and torsos. When the door doesn't open immediately, George instantly knows that Tommy is having trouble with the door handle. Even if the respective apparatus of different companies are of the same make and model, they all have individual characteristics that are unique. Door handles do not always work the same way.

Realizing this in a fraction of a second, George reaches the handle and both he and Tommy bail out, heads first. It is six feet to the pavement. George lands on his head and cracks the back of his head open. It will have to be stitched in the shape of a "Z." He is rendered unconscious. Tommy lands a short distance from George, but remains conscious on the ground and can see what is happening around them.

The officer and chauffeur of Engine 93 see the molotov cocktail thrown, so they move out fast, not knowing that it has gone into the rear compartment and two of the men have exited the rig while it was still moving.

They have come into a riotous situation with people who have prepared molotov cocktails to be thrown at the police. The first fire apparatus onto the block is the first target of opportunity.

Tommy will tell me later that people who were part of this riot continued to throw things at them as they lay in the street. The video on the news will show what looks like burning debris in the street and rioters still heaving objects at it. The burning debris is Tommy and George, badly burned and injured on the ground.

Tommy crawls to George, thinking that if they are going to die here, they are going to die together.

Ladder 45 turns into the block of rioters and they see the burning debris in the street.

The men of 45 Truck are some big powerful men—Brian Jones, Joe Byrne (an FDNY hockey player), Cliff Stabner (a former probie of mine), Mike Wunder (the detail from 36 Truck), and Patty Barr (a former Marine heavyweight boxer who has been coaching George for the upcoming Police/Fire fights). The officer is Lieutenant William Oehm. These are good men.

As the men of 45 Truck come around the corner, they know they have come into a senseless, charged, and dangerous situation. People are still throwing things at the two firemen who have been set aflame. In the middle of this orgy of violence, the truckmen without hesitation scoop up Tommy and George, and speed off to Presbyterian Hospital. George is in agony in the front seat, placed between the chauffeur and the officer, who give him encouragement as they speed on. Tommy is squeezed in with the four men in the rear compartment, getting the same encouragement to hang in there.

The burns are mostly second degree with some third degree and are too severe for Presbyterian, so the burned firemen are quickly transferred to the Burn Center at New York Hospital, where they will be for a while and continue to revisit for the next year.

Tommy and George are a dirty mess, even after all this care. They will have to be brought up to the burn unit to be scrubbed and endure that most excruciating first process, before being dressed and bandaged up properly.

They are both brought upstairs while we all wait downstairs through the dark early hours. A suite in a hotel around the corner has been set up for us and it is about time for a break from all of this. We are told that Tommy and George will probably be asleep by now.

We leave the hospital to go around the corner to the hotel suite, which has been arranged between Jimmy Curran, my friend and president of New York Firefighters Burn Center Foundation, and Mike Carter, the vice president of the Firefighters Union.

It is a big, comfortable suite that we would have enjoyed at another time. We appreciate this comfortable spot at this time to get some rest before we deal with the day ahead of us.

While everyone is settling down, I'm thinking, "One person may be able to get one last peek at the wounded men." I'm the father of one of them and a fire officer myself, so I feel this may hold some sway in getting me into the burn unit to see them one more time before I retire.

Mary Lou is helping to settle Maria, Erika, and Leif, so I take my leave to go back around the corner to see if the burn unit people will let me see them. It is just about dawn and the unit is at its quietest time and I am in luck that these strict and serious people let me in for a couple of minutes.

I put on the essential sterile paper hat, gown, booties, and mask and go into the room where my son and his friend are dead to the world from exhaustion and morphine. They have already gone through a horrible ordeal, but at last they are asleep.

Here are these two big-hearted, strong firemen who would risk everything to save someone, laid low by some criminals. They are a pitiful sight with their arms, their hands with fingers separated by gauze, and their heads all bandaged. It is very quiet in here after all the excitement of the night. They look like a pair of mummy bookends, except for the small involuntary tremors, which come from chills that are the result of the room being so cool compared to their wrapped warm burns. Daylight is just dawning on the East River, which I can see through their window. This is extremely sad, as I stand quietly looking at them. I am thinking of what happened to these two innocent life savers. I make an analogy in my mind that this is like someone stopping to help someone change a flat tire and the person being helped hits the person who stopped over the head. This is not the way rescuers expect to be hurt.

I'm thinking as I leave, with all that can and does happen to firemen, this is the unthinkable.

On September 11, 2001, the unthinkable would occur on such an immense scale that the resulting grief would be beyond measure. Three hundred and forty-three firefighters of the FDNY, 23 police officers of the NYPD, and 37 officers of the Port Authority of New York and New Jersey would die, along with almost 2,600 civilians—all innocents, lost to unfathomable barbarity.

As I leave Tommy and George's room, I realize that this is only the beginning of their ordeal. We have all, suddenly and drastically, had our lives changed by someone's thoughtless act. Tommy Brannigan was to have moved into his new house with his young wife and family today.

Because I am also in the FDNY, they are going to assign me to the needs of my son. When a fireman is badly hurt and needs extended care, someone is assigned to look after his needs and help the injured man and his family. I will be that person for George, while also watching out for Tommy.

On Monday morning, George has to be scrubbed and the dead tissue has to be removed from the second-degree burns, along with the third-degree destroyed tissue. If I'm going to be a caregiver, I feel I have to be here for this. This is done by one of those wonderful burn unit nurses in a water closet with a shower that is used for this purpose. It is very small and thankfully, has just enough room for two. I will have to stay outside.

I am just a couple of feet away outside, so I can hear everything going on inside as the necrotic tissue is removed. This is agony for the burn victim, but it must be done. I hear the most agonizing moans of pain from our former Marine son, who once wrestled in the Marine Corps with a broken neck. It is a torture to witness this, never mind being the person on whom it is being performed. Tommy will have to undergo the same treatment.

Tommy and George are lucky in that Dr. Michael Madden is the burn surgeon who will be taking care of them and overseeing their rehabilitation, which will go on for the next year. George's third-degree burns can be handled without skin grafts. Tommy is not as lucky. He will have to have skin grafts on his hands.

Many firefighters and family members will come to visit in the burn unit. The nurses and doctors allow it because Tommy and George can handle it. As bad as their burns are, they do not cover an area of their skin surface that would prevent visitation or limit it to a great degree. The burn staff can rule with an iron fist when necessary.

Unfortunately, their war won't end when Tommy and George leave the burn unit. There are always others coming in.

The love firefighters develop toward each other manifests itself in many different ways, as the result of their many colorful personalities. In these situations, there are surprises. Friends and family of Tommy and George and friends of mine in the FDNY are coming and going all the time, overseen by the ever-present burn unit nurses, who will not let things get out of hand. They keep control, as they must.

On Sunday morning, when family and friends are in the room, one of George's officers comes to see him. This officer is senior and George has the highest respect for him. They play racquetball and have seen a lot of action together. George thinks he is a cool, smart guy. George and Tommy now have the bandages off their faces, but their faces are badly swollen from the burns. Right now, they are not the nice-looking, handsome guys they were before. They are hardly recognizable. The officer is led to George's side. This tough man starts to cry and swear at those who did this. He is in such psychological pain at the sight of George that the swearing continues through his tears. Another lieutenant, Jay Fischler of Rescue 1, gently leads him away until he can recover enough for a less tormented visit. He recovers just fine. This uncontrolled verbal rage, which is the result of real love, will endear this officer to us forever.

Sunday afternoon, complete lobster dinners are sent to the hospital for Tommy and George from a very thoughtful benefactor in Texas. The nurses have cracked the lobster and made the pieces bite-sized, along with the rest of the meal. The boys are hungry. The burn center people say this is common because of the amount of burn trauma they have endured.

Their heavily bandaged hands and arms make them as awkward when they're eating as a toddler handling utensils for the first time. Holding the knives and forks between the thumb and forefingers, they look like they have never done this before. As pathetic as it is, we all see some humor in this. The struggle is worth it because they are re-

Another Phone Call

ally enjoying this culinary delight, the result of a kind anonymous donor.

One night, Mike Daly from the *Daily News* comes to the hospital to interview George for a column he is writing. Mike does human-interest things and has always given police and firemen a fair shake. He is respected and trusted, so George agrees to an interview. I tell Mike that my son is on morphine and often sleepy. Mike says he would like to try the interview anyway. George is somewhat out of it and a bit spaced out. Whenever Mike asks George a question, George ponders it with slowness and closes his eyes like he is going to sleep. Somehow, through this dopiness, he gets an answer out. Mike then asks George, "What is it that you love about the fire department?" George closes his eyes because he is really out of it, and it looks like there won't be an answer. He opens his eyes and leans forward and answers, "The men." Mike Daly's column will reflect this.

While George and Tommy are still in the hospital, there is a steady flow of visitors from 93 Engine, 45 Truck, Rescue 1, and many other companies. Among these is Battalion Chief Ray Downey, one of the great experts on collapse and who, along with Captain John Cerato, developed the collapse program we use to instruct the rescue companies and support trucks at the Fire Academy. Ray will be one of the 343 firefighters to die at the World Trade Center on September 11, 2001.

Many people heap many kindnesses on Tommy and George. They are too many to mention. We could never say enough about Dr. Madden and the burn unit nurses. They are just wonderful in a terribly tough calling.

Police Commissioner Ray Kelly visited Tommy and George the night they were burned. As the commissioner, a former Marine officer, came up to George, George utters, "Semper Fi."

The commissioner responds in kind. The police will treat the attack on the firemen as an attack on the police.

One afternoon, a New York police detective comes in to interview George and Tommy when Mary Lou and I are there. He is a dapper, good-looking guy, with a nice way of speaking to people. His name is Sergeant Bob Maas from the Thirty-Fourth Precinct Detective Squad. He tells us that they are pulling out all the stops to get the perpetrators of this crime. This detective assures us that they will be relentless in the pursuit of those people. The diligence and adeptness of the Thirty-Fourth's Detective Squad will bring the perpetrators to justice. The story of the tracking and capture of these criminals could easily fill a book.

After a week in the Burn Center, George will be able to go home. Tommy will have to stay longer because of the grafts on his hands. Tommy, who was conscious all the time they were on the ground being pelted, will never go back to work in the fire department. He will go back to school and go into another profession.

It will take a year for George to get back to full duty in Ladder Company 44 on Morris Avenue in the South Bronx. He will work five more years, until the damage to his hands starts to affect his ability to hold tools safely. He will have to leave the job he has wanted all his life. On top of this, when he sings he cannot play the guitar as he once did. The burns affect many aspects of his life; before he gets out of the job, he is hobbling to the rig to respond. His life is completely altered by this, except for the constancy of his supportive wife, Maria, and family. The fire department will also take good care of George.

After George was burned, not a day would go by that someone wouldn't ask how our son was. A twist in this is that, while George suffered through this attack and would eventually lose the job he loved as a result of it, it may have saved his life on September 11, 2001.

CHAPTER 22

Fire Ground

As an instructor to probationary firefighters at the FDNY Academy in 1990 and 1991, I liked to tell them of my thoughts on many of our FDNY rescues. I would say, "The brave act is being there. The rescue is running for your life and taking someone else with you."

Ladder 102 is first due truck arriving in front of 119 Waverly Place in the Fort Green section of Brooklyn. Rescue 2 is already there, along with 210 Engine, with which the rescue company is housed. I've got the irons for forcible entry.

The building is part of a row of Victorian brownstone townhouses from the gaslight era. Usually, fire is very obvious when it occurs in these buildings. This is so true that firemen consider fires in these buildings as classic and somewhat predictable.

At this time, March 1, 1972, these once-private dwellings are divided into apartments on each floor or single-room occupancies. There are three or more families in a building that can be three stories high, with no front or rear fire escape. Any rescue to be made must be through the interior stairs or by ladders.

When there is fire in the basement or parlor floor, it is a hairy proposition for truckmen to get through the interior stairs to the bedrooms on the upper floors. This is done with great risk, undertaken while depending upon the engine holding the fire back with a hoseline. The hallway and stairs are usually filled with heavy, acrid smoke from wood and a hundred years' worth of paint and varnish. The live fire often looks like it is being fed by fuel with flame that is yellow, green, and blue.

It is a little before 10:00 p.m., and nothing is showing in the front of the building, which is not usually the case. The telltale is that the engine has a line stretched (an FDNY term for laying out a hoseline) inside. The rescue company is also in there.

Lieutenant Spillane, the can man, and I proceed up the high front steps to the parlor floor and then follow the hoseline to the third or bedroom floor. There is a lot of fire in the rear, with the engine and Rescue 2 engaged back there. As first due truck, this is our floor of responsibility.

Lieutenant Spillane heads there. I'm about to follow him when I hear the officer of Rescue 2 call out at the door to the front bedroom, which is the room above the entrance to the parlor floor. People often get trapped and die in this room, which is, in fireman's parlance, called the "death room." The door is locked and Lieutenant Cole of the rescue is calling for someone to force entry.

I immediately go to the front door, where the rescue officer is. I have the irons, axe, and 10-pound Halligan lockbreaker tool. I swing the adze of the iron into the jamb of the door and lean down to pop open the locked door.

My first impression as we open the door and I slide my axe under it to keep it open is that we have opened a shallow closet with a wall almost at the door entrance. In this case, the wall is trapped, unmoving thick brown and black smoke, forming a wall at the door.

We drop to our knees and crawl into this fully charged room. I am half a second in front of the officer and come upon the supine figure of a huge man. He weighs around 260 or 270 pounds and I am 160. I can't move him and it is awful in here. I immediately leave him for Lieutenant Cole to deal with as I crawl over him to get to the front window in order to smash it out. I am desperate for air because, in 1972, first due truckmen don't wear masks. As I come to a bed in front of the window, the smoke and heat are worse.

Going for the window, I am tangled in some bedding and get on the window side of the bed, pushing it away as I feel down on the floor. Tangled in the bedding is what momentarily feels like two little dolls. They are not dolls and I say, "I think I've got kids here." This is to whoever can hear me. I've still got to get this window out. At the same time, Jack Carney of Rescue 2 comes out of nowhere, over the bed, and scoops up one of the little ones while I complete the task of taking out the glass. I quickly pick up the other child and head back into the hallway, where Jack is already giving mouth-to-mouth to the three-year-old. I have the one-year-old, who is also unconscious. I place her on a little hallway table and gently move her head back to give her rescue breaths. Just as I move her head back, she gasps suddenly, breathing on her own. Both of the little girls are in critical condition, but they will survive. Their forty-five-year-old uncle will not be as fortunate.

Despite heroic efforts at resuscitation by the firemen and later the doctors and nurses, the uncle will not survive. Apparently, trying to save his little nieces cost him his life.

On another night, Ladder 102 has just pulled up to a six-story tenement on Pulaski Street, Bedford-Stuyvesant. We are the first to arrive. There is fire showing out multiple windows on a couple of floors. The building is occupied and people are hanging out many of the windows. There is a man standing by himself on the corbel lintel above the front door. He is about 20 feet above the ground, with fire showing at the windows on either side of him. There is no engine company in yet.

This is one of those times for "all hands on ladders." Bobby Babstock and I raise a portable ladder to the man above the door and get him down while the aerial is being raised to get people who are at some of the higher windows. All hands are busy on ladders and water has not been put on this fire yet.

It is a busy summer night and all the local fire companies have been running to alarms all over the place and consequently they are all out of position when Ladder 102 comes upon this perilous threat to life.

Bobby and I get the man off the corbel above the door and then use the portable ladder to get to a second-floor window that is showing fire at the ceiling, but not down to the floor. By staying low, we can get through to the rear and up the rear fire escape for searches on the upper floors. Conditions up there must be terrible.

Bobby Babstock is my compadre in the company and we function on the same wavelength. He is tough, smart, and aggressive. The two of us scramble over the windowsill and onto the floor, where fire is lapping across the ceiling and out the top of the window we entered. We scramble toward the rear, making a very quick primary search as we go. There is no time to be precise, because there is barely enough time to get to the rear before these rooms light up completely.

In about 20 to 25 seconds, we are at the rear fire escape and start making searches above the fire where we can. The hallway is still impossible to enter due to fire and heavy smoke, so we continue to return to the rear fire escape after our attempts at searches on each floor as we go up. The second due truck company will back us up when they arrive and will do a more thorough secondary search. Time is not on our side, so we are moving quickly. Fire intensity increases exponentially and it can go from being bad to a disaster in a very short time.

As we ascend, other fire companies are coming on the scene and water is now being put on the fire, but the upper floors are still bad. We crawl through and search as many rooms as we can, with great apprehension, always getting back to the rear fire escape for relief.

There are now firemen showing up all over the building, searching and venting as they go. There is the ever-present sound of breaking glass, the pounding of forcible entry at various places in the building, and the sound of power saws on the roof. Engine companies are starting to get their hoselines into position in the hallway and apartments involved in the fire. This is a full-blown second alarm on arrival.

On the fifth floor, Bobby and I have come upon a badly burned 12-year-old girl who is unconscious and may be dead. In the middle of this dark, hot, and smoky place, strewn with burning debris and rubble, we take turns giving her mouth-to-mouth and cardiac compressions. Parts of her badly burned lips come off in our mouths. She is not responding. Any of a number of things are wrong. Besides her terrible burns, she may have been overcome by carbon monoxide or her smoke-ravaged lungs may have been seared by super-heated air. Sadly, she will not survive, despite our efforts.

The loss of life would have been much greater had it not been for the initial laddering by Ladder 102 before water was ever put on this fire.

CHAPTER 23

Eleventh Floor Aerial Rescue

It is 2:13 a.m. on Saturday, February 5, 1972, and we are responding down Lafayette Avenue. It is a bitter cold morning and we know that we have a fire because the call came in as a verbal alarm from someone at the scene, Box 3947.

These are very busy times for the whole FDNY, with a record-breaking amount of fire throughout the city, and especially in Bedford-Stuyvesant, Brooklyn. Busy truck companies like Ladder 102 are riding with six men and an officer due to the heavy fire workload.

When I transferred to Ladder 102 from Engine 230 in 1969, Ladder 102 had a 1962 American LaFrance tiller rig truck, which was typical in the FDNY. It was a 100-foot aerial ladder trailer apparatus with a tillerman steering the back end. Having two men driving one apparatus was a source of accidents, so the city was trying to eliminate them in all but the narrow streets of Greenwich Village, lower Manhattan, and Brooklyn Heights.

I am the outside vent man this morning and I am riding in the front, sitting between the officer and the chauffeur. The rig we have is a Seagrave rear-mount, single-frame ladder truck with the turntable and controls for the 100-foot aerial ladder at the rear. There is no need for a tillerman. The position of men at a fire is still the same, except that now the tillerman position is called the outside vent man. The outside vent man helps the chauffeur to set up the aerial laddering and any laddering of the front and rear of the fire building.

The four men riding in the bucket seats on either side of the diesel engine are the forcible entry team of Jimmy Farley, the irons man, and Tom Caffrey, the can man on one side. Tom, a relatively new man, is a veteran of the 101st Airborne Division and served in Vietnam. On the other side, the primary roofman is Ernie D'Maria, who will eventually write a book, "Fire: A War That Never Ends" about the Waldbaum's fire in Brooklyn, which killed six firefighters and wounded many others, and the stresses and impact on their lives, and the secondary roofman is Wesley Still, also of the 101st Airborne and a wounded Vietnam War veteran.

The officer is Lieutenant Jimmy Spillane and the chauffeur is Jerry Lambert, the senior man who was a veteran infantryman in the Korean War. Jerry was all-city as a high school basketball player and is the perfect size for an athlete, six feet two inches and lean. He is a fast chauffeur as well as a fast thinker. He always seems to know where the fire is going and consequently is always in position to open up in front of the fire. He is also a very funny man and sees all the humor there is in life. He is stone serious this morning as we approach the Lafayette Housing apartment buildings. These are fire-proof buildings that, in most cases, prevent fire from getting from one apartment to the other. However, fire involving the contents can be very intense, with punishing, poisonous smoke.

We are the first company on the scene. As we approach the address we are looking for, Lieutenant Spillane looks up at the buildings. While pointing, he says, "There it is." Fire is roaring out of two windows way up on the eleventh floor of the address we received, 415 Lafayette Avenue. The FDNY Brooklyn dispatcher is notifying us of children trapped behind the fire. As we get closer, we can see people are hanging out windows adjacent to the fire, with heavy smoke pushing out around them.

Without hesitation, Jerry is already taking the big rig onto the walkway going in, while Lieutenant Spillane is telling him to get as close as possible. This is thinking out loud. These Ladder 102 chauffeurs and others like them are probably among the most experienced the world has ever seen. The 100-foot aerial ladder is an extension of their arms, and the placement of the ladder is almost always impeccable.

The walkways are almost too narrow for the truck to get through and they are lined with steel stanchions and chains. We hear the repeated loud thumps of the stanchions being knocked away by the massive bumpers of the powerful diesel rig.

Eleven floors may be beyond the limit of the 100-foot ladder. Jerry gets the rig almost right up against the building in order to lose as little of the ladder's reach as possible.

Lieutenant Spillane exits the rig and confirms that the people are still at the window with smoke blowing out past them, and they are in immediate peril.

Jerry is securing the rig from inside the cab, putting the power take off (PTO) in position to power the 2500-pound steel aerial ladder. I jump out behind Lieutenant Spillane and head to the rear of the apparatus control panel to lower the hydraulic outrigger tormentors, which will stabilize the frame of the truck when the ladder is raised.

When people are hanging out windows with fire and smoke at their backs, the old expression on how to handle this, "All hands on ladders," is an oversimplification.

With large buildings that are fully occupied, there must be interior search and ventilation, as well as the interior attack on the fire.

"All hands on ladders" really means all those that can be spared. Lieutenant Spillane and the forcible entry team of Jimmy Farley and Tommy Caffrey are on their way to the elevators along with the primary roofman, Ernie D'Maria. Normally, Ernie would be going to the roof because "When you've got the roof, you've got the roof." Vertical ventilation is so important that even while people are at the windows and look like they are about to jump, the roofman has to be undeterred by all that he sees and he must get to the roof. The only exception is in large fireproof buildings like these. The roofman may go to the floor above to vent from above and/or make a roof rope rescue. This is what Ernie is about to do.

Under most conditions, Wesley Still, the secondary roofman, would go along with Ernie. His position is the one with the most built-in flexibility and he takes advantage of this with his soldier's instincts. Without as much as a second thought, he is up on the turntable with chauffeur Jerry Lambert.

If the fire is bad enough, these people in the window will jump to their deaths. As the ladder is lifted out of the bed and turned toward the building, Wesley is calling out loudly, pleading with them to stay put and wait until the ladder is in place. They are desperate, and the fear is that they will jump for the ladder with terrible consequences.

Jerry tweaks out every inch of ladder and now it is fully extended and almost straight up. Wesley is on his way up the ladder as I mount the turntable. I have put on a Scott Air Pak mask for the search inside. Jerry says, "You'll never get through those casement windows with the mask." While I am removing the mask, Jerry is on his way up the ladder.

Wesley has gotten to the tip of the ladder, which, because of the steep angle, has one rung above the sill and one even with it. The people at the window are all kids. There are three of them, all girls, ages seventeen, seven, and five. Wesley has gotten them through the top two rungs. He is carrying the five-year-old and guiding the other two. The angle and height make this a treacherous climb for everyone, especially civilian kids who have never done anything like this before. It is dark, freezing cold, and the wind is howling at better than 25 mph.

Jerry reaches Wesley and the three girls near the top. He grabs the seven-year old, holding her close as he negotiates his way down with his athlete's style.

I am on the ladder now, working my way up, having ditched the mask. Jerry comes past me and behind him is the seventeen-year-old, unescorted. The information we have is that another two girls, ages nine and twelve, are still in there somewhere. It is possible that the forcible entry team might not be able to reach them because there is no water on the fire yet. I pass this girl, who is struggling and shivering cold but managing to make her way down. As I pass her, which under any other circumstances I would not do, I offer her encouragement, as I continue up to help in the search from outside. I will search toward the forcible entry team, who are already searching from inside. I pass Wesley and the little one and get to the window. I can't imagine how Wesley got those kids through the rungs of the ladder. I will have trouble getting through them myself to get inside.

As I am figuring out how to get in, Tommy Caffrey has passed the fire in his search of the back bedrooms. The window is fully charged with heavy black smoke as Tommy gets to the window. While he's a slender man, he is also big, which will make it difficult for him to get out. There is an orange glow in back of him of which he is not aware. Sometimes fire follows smoke like this. Without telling him what I see, I tell him to try to get out onto the ladder with me. Heavy smoke is punishing and Tommy's eyes are as big as silver dollars. I've got my hands on his shoulders, trying to help him squirm through the rungs. I am coaxing him and trying to help him fit through and it is not working. I can't believe that I am out here and have him by his shoulders and if he doesn't get through, he might die while I still have my hands on him.

The smoke suddenly lifts a little and now I can see the source of the orange glow. It is an orange globe lamp and I go from a moment of sheer terror to complete and utter relief. Engine 209 is putting the fire out.

The rest of the forcible entry team gets the other two girls who were still in there—five kids saved during one of the highest aerial ladder rescues in FDNY history.

CHAPTER 24

Explosion at a Senior Citizen's Center

One evening, on Manhattan's East Side, a reported explosion has caused a special call for Rescue 1 in addition to the complete first alarm assignment that would normally respond.

As we arrive quickly, we are getting in as if we were part of the original assignment. The two ladder companies are in the process of assessing the situation, but no one seems to know what has happened. The truckmen are starting to fan out into the multi-storied hotel and apartment house. Presently, there is no evidence of an explosion.

We spread through this large building. Nothing has been found yet. As I go into the rear of the building, there is a one-story setback that is being used as a Senior Citizens' Center. Very casually, someone tells me that this is the source of the alarm. However, everyone in here seems to be going on with whatever they were doing when the reported explosion occurred. Nothing rained down on them, so it became business as usual for them.

This person tells me that the explosion took place above them and when nothing else happened, they reported it and stayed where they were. This is a one-story part of the building, so whatever happened is on the roof. Immediately, I head to the main part of the high-rise to get to the second floor in order to find a way out onto the roof of the setback.

Windows at the back of the second floor look out at the roof of the setback. I climb out on the dark roof and my flashlight beam sweeps across a woman lying on her side in a fetal position, with heavy, dark, viscous blood oozing out of her ears, nose, and mouth. Her head is lying in the dark pooled blood that has come from every opening in her head. She is a young woman and, though we don't make the official decision whether someone is dead or not, I have enough experience to know death when I see it.

To make the explosive noise that was reported, she must have landed with tremendous force, as a result of falling from high above. I am now on the radio reporting what I have found to the rescue officer and chief in charge. As I am doing this, a police officer comes through the window and comes to my side. He immediately does the same thing I have done and notifies his fellow officers and superiors. He agrees with me completely that she is certainly dead and there is no reason for heroic effort here.

More fire personnel and police officers are now around us and the police are indicating they know the floor and room from which she fell. She fell from the fourteenth floor and they have their suspicions.

The police escort a young male out onto the setback to identify the woman. He is a suspected drug dealer and the other occupant of the room from which this woman fell.

The police ask him if he knows her and he nonchalantly answers, "Yeah." They ask him if she was in the room with him and he answers again in the same blasé way, "Yeah."

This totally uncaring attitude may not be legal proof of anything but speaks volumes to the police and heightens their suspicions.

The sound the residents in the Senior Citizens' Center heard at this incident will be heard hundreds of times, with much higher magnitude, by people at the World Trade Center on the morning of September 11, 2001, before the buildings came down.

CHAPTER 25

Trains

One night, Rescue 1 is special-called to Penn Station, along with the full first alarm assignment at that box. All the information we have is that there has been an accident involving a person and a train.

When we get there, there is confusion about what has happened and where to go. Our protocol is to respond to the entrance to Penn Station at the concourse under Madison Square Garden. Train personnel will meet us there and direct us to the problem.

My experience with the supervisory, engineering, and technical people for all the utilities, railroads, and transit system has always been good. These people know their respective skills well and are very impressive and knowledgeable. They are always helpful to us.

Penn Station is a labyrinth of tracks, with Amtrak trains coming in from New Jersey and Long Island Railroad trains coming from Long Island, so it is a big and confusing place to pinpoint the problem immediately.

The emergency call made to the fire department once the accident was discovered was very fast. Our response time is about five minutes. That's not much time for gathering full information on what exactly has happened and where. Information is being transmitted by radio and word of mouth by railroad personnel between each other and then to us. That's why there is often some confusion at enormous places like the Pennsylvania Railroad Station.

The slight confusion subsides and we are directed downstairs to the end of the Amtrak Station. We are led to a passenger train that has come from New Jersey. This train uses catenary electricity from a wire above the train; sometimes, as the train comes into New York, it makes use of electricity from the third rail at the bottom.

When there are accidents involving people with trains, it is never clean. Often, the person is dead and outside of the pathos of the tragic end of a life, it is just a matter of getting them out and into a body bag. Still, it is a dirty job. But when the person is still alive, has limbs that have been severed, and is generally suffering from multiple traumas, bleeding profusely, is in shock or approaching shock, it is a whole different story. We are under that train in the grime and grease, working through that and the blood of the victim, placing tourniquets above partially or totally severed limbs. At the same time, we are figuring how to get this mangled person disentangled from the train of which he or she has become a part. I am thinking of this as we walk along the passenger cars toward the accident site.

At another time, at Grand Central Railroad Terminal, we are taking a similar walk on a platform along a row of passenger trains, but it is during the early morning commuting hours. We are walking along, looking for the reported accident, and there, suspended three feet above the platform, stuck between a massive pillar and the train, is a middle-aged man, his eyes open, his skin bluish in color, and his tongue bulging out—instant death. It is just a matter of jacking the train slightly away from the pillar to release and lower the dead man. The train had been coming to a stop and this man had proceeded to step down off the train, facing the rear, as he may have done every day. The mass of a train just coming to a stop lodged this man between it and the pillar, crushing him to death instantly.

Even though we have seen many of these types of things, it is never routine or something to which you get accustomed. Some of the things that happen to unfortunate human beings are awful, but we are firemen and we deal with it.

At Penn Station, as we get to the passenger car where the accident victim is supposed to be, we are told that the person is on the roof of the train. There is a catenary on top of the train with the overhead wire. There are eleven thousand volts up there and it is so hot you could cook eggs on the top of that train. The electric has been cut at this spot, but it is still considered "hot" until the "A" men come from the railroad.

The "A" men are specially trained linemen whose specialty is grounding the catenary wire on each side of where work must be done where people may have to touch the wire. These guys are professional and serious. They run ground poles down from the catenary wire on each end of the passenger car. When they are done, they run their gloved hands along the one-inch-thick copper catenary wire to assure us it is safe.

Captain Brian O'Flaherty tells me to go on top to check the victim. We place a portable ladder against the passenger car and I climb onto the roof. There is not a lot of room. It is warm up here and I still don't want to touch the wire that has been rendered safe by these confident and competent "A" men.

A young man, twenty-one years old, is lying on his stomach. He is black as coal; when I touch him, he is hot and feels like cardboard. I confirm to the captain that the victim is certainly dead. As I look closely at this face, I can see he has Caucasian features. Whatever possessed him to get on top of that car has killed him.

This poor guy climbed up on the roof of the catenary car when it was disengaged from the overhead wire and apparently running on its third rail capability. When the train switched from third rail to the overhead catenary, he was killed instantly and then cooked until he was literally mummified—a terrible, sudden end of a life.

CHAPTER 26

Diving—Blackwater

It is black, black, black—zero visibility. A little boy has fallen into a manhole 25 feet inland from where I am. This is the foot of Tiffany Street at Hunt's Point on the East River. I am in 30 feet of deep water, trying to determine what kind of opening I am going into to reach the manhole. I am very guarded. It is no place for imagination.

It is April 30, 1989, and I have been diving for around six years. I have just gotten over Hepatitis A and I don't know if I want to continue diving, but here I am. The special call came in as a child falling into a sewer and I am not thrilled about this situation. However, I am the primary diver, the first one in the water. Joe Angelini is my backup today. Joe will be killed along with his son Joe Jr. on September 11, 2001, at the World Trade Center when the towers collapse.

When we get there, Rescue 3, not a dive team, already has one of their men in a Narwhal neoprene suit down in the manhole. We think the little boy might be in the water conduit, which is a large pipe or a tunnel that goes to the East River. This is what I am attempting to enter. At least this is not a sewer, but it is not a lot better, because it is the drainage for all the gutters of the streets in the vicinity. It is very dirty water, which accounts for much of the darkness.

To get to this point we have had a few problems. The nonexistent visibility prevents me from just swimming to the opening. Tommy Baker places a 20-foot-long, wooden-handled pull-down hook onto the top of the opening of the drainage pipe or tunnel. Then, proceeding down that pole, I get tangled in a bunch of fishing line; I can't go up or down and my head is barely out of the water. Harvey Harrell, who will also be killed at the World Trade Center on September 11, 2001, has to cut me free of that mess. So here I am, at the entrance to the unknown.

Luckily, at this point in time, we divers are tethered to someone on the deck above and I have hard-wire communication with a bone ear microphone behind my ear. It's very comforting to be able to communicate with someone above. The only sound I can hear is the rushing water passing by my ears, under the hood, running from the drainage pipe to the East River. It is a constant flowing sound.

I hear Danny Killoran ask me, "Have you found the opening?" I tell him I have and that I am on the lip of it at about 30 feet down. He tells me there are two police divers in the water and that they will try to contact me. That is good to know, as I can't see anything. It won't be a surprise when I am bumped in the dark. Danny says, "The police divers are not going in, but they are checking on you and will just let you know they are there." It's also comforting to know someone else is in this black water with me. These police divers are very good and, in moments, one of them has made contact with me and grabs my hand with assurance. I am impressed at how fast they have found me. They are untethered and searching outside the drainage. I am making my way toward the manhole, hoping to find the little boy.

On the lip of the drainage, which is a stone sill, I am trying to determine how wide this opening is. I move to the left to determine the wall to my left. From there, I ease myself to the right, floating, just off the bottom. It is inky black and my dive light is useless, as is the case in most water around New York at depths beyond 20 feet. Extending my arms out to the side, I float sideways to the wall on the right. My spread arms are between five and six feet wide. I figure the width of the opening is 10 feet across and about 10 feet high—sort of a big garage door opening in size.

I am looking for a little boy in a very big space. Chances are, if he is still in this drainage, he is on the bottom and that is my immediate concern. Now to move further in. Normally in searches on the bottom, we swing arcs back and forth, letting out a couple of feet of tether at the end of each arc, slowly searching further and further as tether line is let out. This cannot be done as I move into this tunnel. Even though I am tethered, I have no point of reference in front of me. With the tether above and in back of me, I go forward toward the uncovered manhole into which the little boy has fallen.

Even during searches at fires, we are always searching for "a newborn infant." Just as I am trying to figure out how to make sure I don't miss anything, my hand comes upon a 20-pound cobblestone, also known as Belgian block. I push the cobblestone an arm's length in front of me along the right side wall. I am now moving the stone a couple of feet to my left, all the time searching by feel alone along the bottom. After a couple of movements of the stone to the left, I am at the left wall again. I slide the heavy stone forward along the left wall, a couple of feet and then I shift the stone to my right until I get to the right side wall again. Moving the cobblestone forward, then sideways and then forward again I am covering ground and not missing anything as I move along. I am forming my own grid pattern with the cobblestone as my point of reference.

The water that is rushing toward the East River is giving me the sensation of swimming upstream. It takes time to cover a grid in this large tunnel and I am in about 10 feet, when Danny's voice comes through the speaker microphone on my mastoid bone, tucked in behind my ear, saying, "They've got the kid." I am immediately relieved. It is good that they have got the little boy and that is primary. Also, I am glad to be able to get out of this blackness.

Richie Evers, one of the senior men of Rescue 2 and someone with whom I attended Commercial Divers' Institute, found the little boy about 25 feet upstream, further inland from the open manhole.

When I emerged from the water, the word was that they could not revive the eight-year-old. Pathetically, the local people were elated at what they thought was a rescue but had actually turned out to be a recovery. Just think—someone had covered an open manhole with cardboard and a little boy, playing with his friends, stepped on it and fell through to his untimely death.

In 1983, when the scuba teams of Rescue Company 1, Manhattan, and Rescue Company 2, Brooklyn, were formed, Department Order No. 97 designated the teams for "in water firefighting" with a 24-hour capability. The impetus for this formation was a July 1981 pier fire at Seventeenth Street and North River, which is the Hudson River. The pier was one hundred feet wide by one thousand feet long, built of heavy timber. The substructure continued to burn deep underneath and could not be reached by hose streams from above. The fire continued to simmer under the pier for three weeks, constantly emitting acrid smoke from the under-pier timber, which was saturated with creosote. The smoke drifted all over the Lower West Side of Manhattan. There were many complaints from the citizens who lived and worked there. As Manhattan and Brooklyn had a lot of commercial waterfront, Rescue 1 and Rescue 2 were given the training and equipment for scuba diving, primarily for under-pier fires. This would turn out to be very effective.

The initial basic dive training was at Aqua-Lung Dive School of New York run by Fran Garr, a noted and respected dive instructor. We dove with wet suits and standard mouthpiece regulators, a combination with which I was very comfortable.

On Wednesday, March 3, 1982, before we have completed our basic diving certification, Tommy Prin, Norman Newkirk, and I are in the water with just our wet suits, booties, gloves, fins and masks, at a second alarm, Box 651, for Pier 54 at Fourteenth Street and North River. Our eagerness and enthusiasm have outweighed all other considerations. We are the first members of Rescue 1 to swim under a pier fire. The air and river water temperatures are 28 degrees, as moving water can be below freezing. I am amazed at how comfortable I am. My wet suit is three-eighth-inch thick, with a synthetic terry-like lining. There is no shock as the cold water fills the tight space between my skin and the wet suit and instantly warms to my body temperature. There is no way we will pass up this opportunity as long as there is no direct order not to. As it turns out, there is not that much fire underneath the pier, but at least it gets us into the water under real-life conditions.

On June 4, 1982, there is a special call for Rescue 1 to an all-hands working fire at East River and 118th Street. We are encountering a lot of traffic coming uptown and the FDR Drive along the East River is backed up to downtown Manhattan. As we get to the pier at 118th Street, the fire is out of control, with heavy fire and smoke coming out from under the pier. It is now a second alarm and the Manhattan Borough Chief wants us in the water now. Paddy Brown and I go into the water. This is the pier of the Washburn Wire Works, which is a large building on top of the pier. There is a lot of fire in the heavy timber and wood sleepers underneath the pier above us. We place an eight-foot length of rope looped over the nozzle to be wrapped around pilings, keeping Paddy and me from being driven back from the reaction as we open the nozzle. We drive water up into the burning substructure of the pier. We leap frog each other from bay to bay and piling to piling, handing the nozzle and hoseline back and forth to each other as we go along. In a very short time, just the two of us extinguish a second alarm fire under that pier that could have gone on for days or more. The chief was ecstatic and impressed. This was the very reason for the existence of the FDNY dive teams. Paddy Brown will be killed as the captain of Ladder Company 3, along with all his men, at the World Trade Center on September 11, 2001.

Eventually, through experience, we all realized that we were being exposed to some nasty water, even though I liked getting in the water with a wet suit and fins to scoot around in the water unencumbered by heavy tanks with 80 cubic feet compressed air. The solution was going to be putting us in dry suits with hoods and enclosed facepieces with the air supply from those large, heavy tanks.

In the summer of 1982, a couple of divers from both Rescue 1 and Rescue 2 came down with amebiasis, which more than likely came from diving in polluted water. Both companies were completely taken out of service and all members were tested and examined. Most of us turned out to be healthy, but the services of a nationally recognized expert would be used to choose equipment to dive dry.

That expert was Walt Hendrick, who ran "Lifeguard Systems" at Commercial Divers' Institute, Whitestone, Queens. Walt and his father before him were Navy scuba divers with probably as much underwater time as anybody in the world.

Walt Hendrick is a thorough and serious instructor. He always seemed to know everything that was happening on deck, as well as everything that was going on in the water, no matter how many divers were in the water. That included those standing by as emergency divers.

To protect us from exposure to pollutants in the water, Walt trained us in the use of the full facepiece, hard-wire voice communications, and lightweight dry suits that could be worn over insulated underwear when it was frigid. He trained us in "blackwater" advanced search and rescue methods. The training included team operations of Rescue 1 and Rescue 2 together. Tethering of the divers was stressed and I believe that this could save the life of a rescue diver. We were also taught underwater signaling with just a rope tether and no voice communication. Walt made sure we were thoroughly trained in team rescue and self-rescue. He would always apprise us of any dive accidents that had recently occurred to drive home his emphasis on safety at all times. This is the way it was going to be.

The deepest water around New York City is around 60 feet and that would be the middle of the Hudson River. In the daytime, if submerged deeper than 20 feet, there was zero visibility. At night, there was just about no visibility at any depth. It is no exaggeration that it is called "blackwater." After a while, my dive light was an afterthought that I could use to identify an object at six inches away at the most.

The eagerness with which we all took to diving in the dirty "blackwater" led Walt Hendrick to say, "I have never seen so many men in one place so willing to go into that type of water." My own thoughts on it were that the FDNY firemen are so used to wearing masks and spend so much time in dark places that the big difference is that diving is wet and cool, and better than a lot of other places we had all been in.

While at Commercial Divers' Institute, we even got to go down six atmospheres in a recompression chamber, in case we ever needed recompression.

There were many real-life dives and many drill dives. Most times, we dove dry with the full facepiece and sometimes, for speed into the water, we dove wet, but almost always with the full facepiece, with or without voice communication.

At ten o'clock on a Sunday night, Rescue Company 1 gets a special call to Fourteenth Street and North River. It is May 20, 1984. A car is in the water. I am the primary diver and to get dressed fast, I am in a wet suit with a standard regulator. We get there quickly.

We have a reliable source and he is the engineer on duty for FDNY Marine Company 2, which is berthed there. I get into the water, don my fins, and inflate my buoyancy compensator (BC) enough to float me. I am on my side as I kick my fins to the location to which the marine engineer has directed me. I release the air from the BC and submerge 15 feet to the top of a car. If it is the right car, I am right on the money, owing to the reliable source. However, I cannot tell what type of car it is.

I have a light that is on but useless. I swim around the car and it is locked with all windows closed. I ascend to get a Halligan tool to break the side tempered-glass windows and also bring a line with a float attached so the other divers can find the car and me if need be. The other divers are Jack Boyle and Dick Martinsen. Both are good men in the water.

I submerge a second time and tie the line to the side mirror, with my face six inches away from it, so I can see it. The water resistance makes it hard to swing the Halligan tool. After a couple of attempts, the side window disintegrates soundlessly, yielding to the point of the Halligan. I pull the door lock, but I cannot open the door by myself, because one-third of the car is in bottom silt. I reach inside onto the front seat as far as I can feel. With the tank on my back I cannot fit through the window. I feel from the floor and front seat to the roof. Then I reach across the roof to the back and then down to the rear seat. I reach down further and on the floor I feel a mature male, supine. I cannot get enough leverage to get him out. I ascend a third time to let the others know that it is the right car and what I have found.

Boyle and Martinsen are in the water immediately. Both are strong men. Jack is my size, but Dick is a powerful and muscular 250-pound, six foot one inch Norwegian. We all get down to the car, where it is black and all feel. Bumping into each other, it is arms and legs to the side of the head, as we are all working to open the door. Jack and Dick are fresh, so I try to make way for them to get the supine man out as they get the door open. The two of them get him out and ascend with him. Resuscitation fails and the rescuers cannot revive him.

Later, we will find out that this man had been at the Annual Ninth Avenue Fair in the afternoon and accidentally drove off the pier to drown, at ten o'clock that night. Maybe if the water had been colder, we might have saved him.

On August 23, 1985, at around seven p.m., Rescue Company 1 is special-called to Marine Company 6 on Grand Street and the East

River. The port engine of the Fireboat "Alfred E. Smith" is not producing enough revolutions per minute to respond. The Marine Company's problem cannot be resolved by the marine division for a couple of days.

The chief engineer has determined that something is wrapped around the port propeller shaft and it is evident that the shaft will have to be examined by a dive team. The concern is that damage can be done to the port engine.

Captain O'Flaherty, Rescue 1, has me dive under the fireboat to see what is wrapped on the shaft. There is a swift East River current, so I have to wrap one arm around the propeller shaft to keep from being torn away and inadvertently surfacing. I am diving in a wet suit with full facepiece and hard-wire communication.

At first, nothing is obvious, so I check the propeller blades on both props, and find that five of the six three-foot blades are bent and rounded at the tips. On further examination of the shaft, I find that what had at first looked like shaft way packing between the shaft way and the port propeller, is actually two-inch nylon hauser rope, burned onto the shaft, where it looks almost like a part of it that belongs there.

Mike Fitzgerald, who will eventually be our son George's lieutenant in Ladder 44 and then a captain, comes into the water and under the hull of the Fireboat Smith to help with what I've found.

We are both hanging onto the shaft with one arm while the strong current pins us to the bottom of the hull of the 100-foot boat. The first attempts at cutting the nylon hauser that's so tightly wrapped and burned onto the shaft with our dive knives are fruitless. I ask for a hacksaw and they send one down to us. Mike and I take turns cutting through the nylon, which is so tight that when we finally get through, the blackened nylon rope looks like a bushing that has always been part of the shaft. This job has taken about one hour and we are able to put a 100-foot fireboat, the "Smith," back in service for the time being. A letter of appreciation from the captain of Marine 6 followed this.

On October 22, 1986, the helicopter with traffic reporter Jane Dornacher, piloted by William Pate, went down into the slip on the north side of the Aircraft Carrier Intrepid Air Museum. Rescue Company 1 responded.

In the two minutes it takes for us to go from the quarters of Ladder 21 and Engine 34, I am dressed in a wet suit and full facepiece, fins, and buoyancy compensator. Paul Hashagen is the other diver, who is dressed the same way.

The helicopter is submerged in 25 feet of water. As I get onto the ladder leading into the water, I slip my fins on and somebody pulls the tabs to my full facepiece and a main tab breaks. I have to switch to a standard regulator. In that short time, Paul Hashagen is in the water, diving on the helicopter. He quickly surfaces with Jane Dornacher, hands her off to others of us in the water and dives again for the pilot. Almost as quickly, he surfaces with the pilot.

Meanwhile, I am tying the lifeless body of Jane Dornacher to a rope that will pull her up the 10 feet to the dock. I follow and work on her, giving her heart compressions while someone else is administering breaths with the use of an air bag. It is to no avail; however, the pilot will live.

At this time, I was an experienced diver and ready for this dive. When I had trouble, a guy like Paul Hashagen would fill that hole fast. He got both victims out and saved the life of the pilot. Ironically, Danny Killoran, who would normally have been checking on me, was on his way into work for the night tour and actually heard Jan Dornacher's alarm as the traffic helicopter went down.

CHAPTER 27

The Movies

Dick Martinsen, while still a member of Rescue 1, started acting in local plays. He then expanded to a couple of musicals that were performed by FDNY personnel and friends to benefit the New York Firefighters Burn Center. Jimmy Curran, who was a lieutenant in Rescue 1 and the president of the Burn Center Foundation, handled the promotion of those musicals.

The "acting bug" had bitten Dick and eventually led to professional acting, acting schools, and a serious interest in the acting profession. His work in New York involved him in soaps and some film work. He became a member of the Screen Actors Guild and was kept quite busy.

Dick is a handsome, blond Norwegian, powerfully built and an impressive-looking man, with an ingratiating personality. This last trait probably had a lot to do with how well he got along with people in show business, which in turn kept him busy. His face popped up in many magazine ads, as well as many television commercials. We never knew when his face would appear on television or billboards.

Along the way, as he got more exposure to his acting craft, he met directors and producers who had parts for extras as firemen. Dick convinced them that he could get as many real firemen as they needed and it would be cheaper in the long run because the firemen could supply their own fire clothing at no expense to the film company. The firemen would look authentic because they were. This made sense to directors and producers and the door was open for us firemen to play firemen extras in the movies.

In the summer of 1985, a number of us were given jobs as extras in a Charles Bronson movie, "Death Wish 3." Charles Bronson would be walking down a street of bedlam as various fires were taking place in buildings along his way down the street. This was a run-down area of East New York, Brooklyn. Our job was to ride a fire engine down the street past Charles Bronson as he walked along. We didn't know if this was the beginning of the movie or the middle or the end.

In the course of the day, we make 10 to 12 passes like this. All the time, there are other scenes taking place.

The film companies always cater a wonderful lunch or dinner for everyone working on the set. In this case, it was set up in a vacant lot, next to derelict buildings. They set up banquet tables for all the workers, staff, and extras. The star and directors had separate tables that were exclusive to them. It was very nice treatment.

Often, there was "standing by" time, when we could watch the close-up shots being taken of the star, Charles Bronson. He was a rugged-looking man. He would walk by doing his part as if we weren't there.

There was a busy local engine company of the FDNY also standing by with hoselines stretched because live fire was used in these scenes. The fire was controlled and emanated from propane tanks engineered by pyrotechnic professionals. In the movie scenes, it would look like real structural fires. The engine company was stationed there as a precaution.

As a rule, on the set of a movie, every extra for any occupation or position looks exactly like what he or she is supposed to be in the part. Even standing among them, you almost believe they are whatever they appear to be—the utilities people, the construction workers, the cops, etc. All look real until you speak to them and they give you a blank look. It is all make believe.

The local real engine company standing by has a particular interest in us, because we look as real as they are. They can see the blue frontpiece on my helmet with the big "1" on it, denoting Rescue 1. Another helmet has a red frontpiece with a big "4" on it, denoting Ladder 4, mid-town Manhattan. As far as the engine company goes, these are just props.

I cannot resist telling these real firemen that we are real firemen playing movie firemen. They are incredulous at first, but come to realize it is the truth. We are the only people on the set actually playing who we really are. The irony of it all is that we are being paid more than these firemen performing their real role.

When the movie was completed and I saw it, our ride down the street was not to be seen. I said to Dick Martinsen, "Whatever happened to that scene of us driving down the street past Charles Bronson?" Dick's answer was, "Did you read the credits at the end?"

Just before Christmas 1988, Bill Murray and Dan Akroyd were shooting scenes for "Ghostbusters II" in lower Manhattan. They hired a bunch of us as firemen extras. It would turn out that this was for the last scenes of the movie.

For three frigid nights, we worked close to Bill Murray and Dan Aykroyd. We even had a couple of firemen reprimanded for "over acting."

A massive building with twin marble spiral stairs on lower Whitehall Street was the scene of the museum in the movie. The perimeter of this building follows the lines of the original Dutch settlement of Peter Stuyvesant, south of Wall Street. We rested out of the cold with our boots off and ate wonderful catered meals here. The experience was terrific and the pay was good with Christmas on the way.

In the 1990s, I even got to be a technical adviser in a small movie to combat drunk driving. The movie required extricating auto accident victims with the use of the Hurst tool, the "Jaws of Life," for which I was an instructor. This movie was filmed in Fort Tryon Park, Washington Heights in Manhattan, but it was supposed to be a country road in Virginia.

Who could have imagined, in the middle of a career of twenty-eight thousand alarms, there would be movies, too?

CHAPTER 28

The FDNY Chaplain

Walking up Fifth Avenue, with its thousands of people passing by, I notice a tall Irish man walking south. What makes him noticeable is the way is he is dressed and that he is not in a particular hurry.

It is mid-September and the Steuben Day Parade is today. I am on my way up to see it. It is a beautiful warm day. The sun is shining brightly. This man I'm noticing is wearing a dark blue FDNY T-shirt and baseball hat. I'm thinking he is an old fireman by his looks, casualness, and the way he seems to be taking in everything around him. He is older, but still a handsome-looking guy. Just as my thoughts go back to where I am heading, this man makes a deliberate diagonal move across the sidewalk and bumps into me. Suddenly, my brain has caught up and I recognize Father Mychal Judge, the FDNY Catholic Chaplain. He laughs as he grabs my arm.

There are millions of people on any day in this city, so recognizing someone is always a surprise and a delight. The way Father Judge is dressed has completely thrown me off and the two of us get a laugh about it. Usually, I see him in his brown Franciscan robe and sandals or his chaplain's "Class A" chief's uniform. We are friends. He will continue on his way, taking in Manhattan and I will go see the Steuben Day Parade.

Father Judge succeeded his good friend, Father Julian "Jules" Deacon, who was a very beloved chaplain for the FDNY. Mychal Judge would become a much-beloved chaplain in his own right.

St. Francis of Assisi Church and Friary are across West Thirty-First Street from the quarters of Ladder 24 and Engine 1. Father Julian often would come in for a cup of coffee, stand in his Franciscan robe and sandals, smoking his cigarette, holding it in a European fashion. He would be ministering without even knowing it. He was a fire buff who took in many fires and became the sentimental favorite to be the Catholic Chaplain. When he died of cancer, his wish was to be replaced by his friend Father Mychal Judge, who did not know much about the fire department at that time. He would learn fast and become very involved with the fire personnel and their families. Over the years that he was the chaplain, our paths would cross many times, like pleasant ships in the night—a few words exchanged and then on our own ways. Mychal Judge was a busy man.

Early on, when he was a new chaplain, he was invited to dinner with Engine 93, Ladder 45 and Rescue 3 at their quarters on West 181st Street. At that time, our son George was a fireman in Engine 93.

After dinner, there is a lull. Father Judge is sitting there quietly because he really doesn't know these men yet and he is just beginning to become familiar with the fire department. George says, "Father, would you like to see the rigs and what is on them?" Father Judge replies, "Of course." It is a chance for a close look at what is on those trucks.

While George takes Father Judge around the trucks and shows him the varied tools and appliances, he says to him, "Father, if cops became priests, they would be Jesuits. If firemen became priests, they would be Franciscans." The chaplain likes this analogy.

As a result of this visit and tour, a friendship is created that will remain for the rest of Mychal Judge's life. The friendship between George and Father Judge will eventually extend to me and then our whole family.

Father Mychal Judge baptized Maria and George's first-born daughter, Gabrielle. From that time on, whenever I ushered at fire department funerals with my boss, another favorite uncle, the wonderful battalion chief, Pietro "Pete" Valezano, Father Judge would always ask, as he passed by going out of the church, "How is our little girl?" It didn't matter whether it was St. Patrick's Cathedral or a lesser-known church.

Mychal Judge would give the most touching homilies to the families of the deceased, as he addressed each grieving family member, especially the wife and each individual child. His ease and grace were as comforting as his soft words.

If a fireman was killed suddenly, Father Judge would go to the family immediately to offer what comfort he could give. In some terrible ordeals where a fireman was burned badly and fighting for his life in the burn center, Mychal Judge would make visits at all hours, by himself. At the same time, he would be involved with the fireman's family, comforting them to whatever degree they needed or wanted. This graceful man had the common touch.

He married our daughter Erika and our son-in-law Martin. On the anniversary of their marriage, he would send a congratulatory note of remembrance to them. I am told he did this for all those couples he married.

For any services he performed for us, I would want to give him something. Mychal Judge would always gladly accept a donation for St. Francis of Assisi Church. He would say, "God knows they can use it." St. Francis of Assisi Church feeds the homeless every day. But I also wanted to give him a personal gift, which was almost impossible. I knew he enjoyed his Irish heritage, so I got him a dark-green wool scarf with understated shamrocks on it, figuring this might cause him to keep it for himself. I also gave him a Rescue 1 FDNY sweatshirt, which he might wear to display his association. The reality of it all is that the scarf probably didn't make it back to the rectory. It was probably given to the first needy person he met. He may have kept the Rescue 1 sweatshirt because it was from Rescue 1, but I wouldn't bet on that either. There probably wasn't a thing in this world that he wouldn't give away.

Any encounters with Father Judge would be brief because I was aware of how busy he was and that his time was precious. He had a large flock.

One time, at the wake of a fireman killed in the line of duty, he pauses next to me for a minute, taking a breather. The place is packed with uniformed firemen, family members, and friends. He says to me, "The firemen handle the death of their own very well." I agree and I give my reason why: "Firemen develop a sense of mortality early in their careers due to the nature of the job with all it entails. Father, I have tried to live every day as if it was my last and by now it has really added up." This makes him laugh.

Another time, we are at the retirement party for John Driscoll of Rescue 1. It is being held in the officer's mess at the Seventh Armory on Park Avenue. During a rare 10 minutes, Father Mychal Judge, Joe Angelini of Rescue 1, and I sit together, just the three of us. We each have a plate of food and have converged on the same table. While eating, I lean back and tell him, "We are more connected than you know." He has a quizzical look on his face. I tell him that his first official act in the fire department was giving Last Rites to a long-time friend of mine, Lieutenant Tommy Williams of Rescue 4. I had known Tommy since we were 18 years old and he was the first fireman I looked for on my first run in the fire department. Father Mychal Judge is taken aback by this.

A favorite quote of Father Judge's:

> "If you want to make God laugh,
> Tell him what you are doing tomorrow."

Mychal's Prayer:

> "Lord, take me where You want me to go;
> Let me meet who You want me to meet;
> Tell me what You want me to say and
> Keep me out of Your way."

Joe Angelini and Father Mychal Judge will both die at the World Trade Center on September 11, 2001. Father Judge will give general absolution to all those there that day before he dies there himself. This beautiful, selfless man will be listed as the first official death of the FDNY on September 11, 2001.

CHAPTER 29

Some of the Men

In my time in the Fire Department New York, from 1964 to 1995, there were so many good men that there are entirely too many to mention them all. It is a department of twelve thousand people, of whom I would know approximately a couple thousand at any time. Personnel changed over a couple of times from World War II veterans to Korean War veterans to Vietnam War veterans, and to Desert Storm veterans.

It is impossible to give a full accounting of all the wonderful people I met and worked with during my 31 years in the FDNY. Many became best friends and even that is hard to tabulate to the degree they deserve.

Any attempt at a list of notable men will always be incomplete, so anyone I knew and respected who is not on this list is just a matter of an oversight.

The few experiences that I describe are mostly to show what it was like to be a fireman in the City of New York in the 136 years before September 11, 2001. All firemen experience unusual things to varying degrees in their careers.

They all face fire and know what it is to crawl into those long, dark, hot places. On 9/11, the survivors would deal with something never dealt with before. All responders to the site of the totally collapsed and burning World Trade Center on that day will never be the same. Innocence was lost. Since 9/11, a dangerous job has been compounded by the ever-present threat of terrorism. Things are very different today.

Henry "Hank" Zuercher—

"The Big Z." "The Swiss Knight." Battalion Chief. Korean War Army veteran. Hank Zuercher deserves a book by himself—an extraordinary fireman in a class by himself. As a fireman in Ladder 108 and Rescue 2, his six foot one inch frame carried 245 pounds of granite muscle. When he was a lieutenant in Squad 3 and I was in Engine 230, the two of us, having been gymnasts, would walk on our hands on the apparatus floor. Later, he was the captain of Ladder 108. He was gifted with the strength and instincts that made him a great fireman. He was an inspiration to the rest of us and was bigger than life as he lived it—one of a kind. In the Old West, he would have been "The Lawman."

Bobby Babstock—

Former Navy radar man, who could write the names of the men who were in on lunch on the blackboard backwards. My compadre in our Ladder 102 days. A philosophical man who loves life. Handsome and well put together, the picture of the fireman. Totally dependable and always in the thick of it. A wonderful man to be around. He would go on to Rescue 4 in Queens while I went to Rescue 1 in Manhattan. Later, he would be a lieutenant in Rescue 2 under Captain Ray Downey and would finish as the captain of Ladder 120 in Brownsville, Brooklyn. A big-hearted man in every sense of the word. Butch Cassidy, as played by Paul Newman, comes to mind when I think of my good friend of many years. We rode to work together.

Tom Zuercher—

Lieutenant Engine 230. Battalion Chief. Tall and handsome, he could fill his brother Hank's boots. However, more often, Hank was filling Tom's boots and getting them wet. They were the only men in the house of two companies, Engine 230 and Squad 3, who wore size 14 boots. At a subway fire, after years of not having seen each other, he was a chief and I was a senior fireman of the Rescue Company and despite the disparity of our ranks, we hugged each other. He said to me, "At least we recognized each other." He still looked good.

*Dennis Cross—

"The Iron Cross." Vietnam Army veteran. Direction-finding operator for U.S. Army Security Agency. Came to Ladder 102 as a lieutenant, promoted out of Ladder 105. We met years before and my impression of him was of an altar boy with curly, light blond hair. We became friends and, while working with him in Ladder 102, I got to know what a great officer he was and almost pulled my transfer paper to Rescue 1 in order to continue working with him. He was a pleasure. Always thinking of how to do it better. Extremely aggressive, yet with a light touch. He would eventually be the captain of Ladder 102 and spend many years there. He used to say he would do 10 years in each rank. He just about did that. As a battalion chief, he became the Battalion Commander of the 57th Battalion, of which Ladder 102 is a part. It was said that his whole career was in one square mile, but what a square mile—Bedford-Stuyvesant, Williamsburg, Brooklyn, "The Borough of Fire." He would never have left the FDNY until he was forced out at the age of 65. On September 11, 2001, he was killed as a result of the terrorist attack on the World Trade Center, as the acting Deputy Chief of the 11th Division, at the age of 59. Our son Leif, as a member of Ladder 102, had the good fortune to work under Chief Cross and knew this wonderful man. He was my friend for 30 years. We rode to work together.

**Brian O'Flaherty—

Captain of Rescue 1, later a battalion chief, a career that paralleled that of his life-long and best friend, Dennis Cross. He was a fireman in Ladder 105 and a lieutenant in Ladder 102 before becoming the captain of Rescue 1. He is one of the few survivors of the World

Trade Center collapse on September 11, 2001. He was badly wounded while his best friend was killed there. Brian and Dennis were friends since they were six years old. Both of their fathers had been firemen and were already dead when they were very young. Dennis's father died in the FDNY as a member of Ladder 131, Brooklyn; Brian's father had been a member of Ladder 105, but went to war in World War II as a pilot and was killed. "Captain Brian O'Flaherty took me to bad places; he was tough and he knew his stuff."

Danny Killoran—

The chauffeur for the rescue captains, Bill Anderson, Tom Baldwin, and Brian O'Flaherty, for a span of 20 years—a reliable and steady man. When I was diving, he helped me get dressed and made sure I had everything. Danny and I spent the night with the Pope. His brother, Joe, was a lieutenant and Joe's two sons, Michael and Jimmy, were firemen. We rode to work together.

Al Heinbach—

Lieutenant in Ladder 102 for 20 of its busiest years. Later promoted to captain. He was "The Boss." He died one week after retiring.

Jim Basile—

Fireman in Ladder 102 for more than 10 years and a lieutenant in Ladder 111 for 20 years, Bedford-Stuyvesant, Brooklyn. Korean War Marine. For real, for real, fearless. When I was the can man (extinguisher man) and he had the irons (forcible entry man), it was an experience never to be forgotten. A legend.

Connie Metzger—

Chauffeur in Ladder 102. Former Army tank driver. Handsome, avid reader, smooth, and intelligent. He was a fourth-generation fireman with the instincts to show for it. He made the most creative use of the aerial ladder under the worst circumstances. He was an extraordinary chauffeur. When Ladder 102 had the tractor and trailer aerial ladder with a tiller, he would always slow down at corner turns and look over his shoulder to make sure the tillerman was okay, getting his back end through. A natural leader.

George Goldbach—

A smart, tough truckman in Ladder 102. He was the first man I ever saw stick his hand through a hole in the roof to see if fire was in the cockloft. If it felt moist there was no fire, but if it was dry there was fire. He was eventually promoted to lieutenant and served as an engine officer in Bedford–Stuyvesant, Brooklyn. After he retired, I was at an emergency at the Waldorf–Astoria Hotel. I was with Rescue 1, waiting at the roof bulkhead for the fire safety director, when the door opened and George and I astonished each other by meeting there. He was the fire safety director. Later on, he would become a Chief Training officer in Colorado and also write technical articles for *Fire Engineering* magazine. A wealth of knowledge and experience.

Jerry Lambert—

All-city basketball player. Korean War infantryman. Very fast chauffeur for Ladder 102. Great instincts for heading off the fire. On my first run to a fire as a tillerman, Jerry turned into a narrow street with double-parked cars. I did get my end through without closing my eyes. Jerry was the chauffeur at the eleventh-floor rescue. An impressive fireman.

Charlie Stressler—

Chauffeur in Ladder 102, former Army Special Forces, and a very fast chauffeur who really enjoyed getting in first. He was the son of Assistant Chief Charles Stressler and never took any advantage of that fact. He took a lot of pride in Ladder 102's American LaFrance truck.

Jim Ellison—

Fireman for many years in Ladder 102. Promoted to lieutenant in Ladder 124 before coming to Rescue 1. He would finish as a captain. Before we had radios, he was on the roof as a roofman for Ladder 102. The 34th Battalion Chief Adolf Tortoriello called up to him on the roof, and asked what they had up there. Jimmy put his arms dramatically straight down at his side and brought them up alongside his body into a straight-out "T," indicating a fully involved cockloft fire. Later, the chief jokingly told Jimmy to never give him a signal like that again. There was another time, at a third alarm school fire, when we were in blinding smoke with Lieutenant Al Heinbach. Pete O'Dea, the senior man, asked where the new kid was. Al Heinbach answered, "He is with Ellison and I am sure he is some place he has never been before." The kid was Steve DeRosa, who would eventually get the James Gordon Bennett Medal, FDNY's highest and oldest medal for bravery, as a member of Ladder 102 and become an Assistant Chief of Department. Jimmy was a superb truckman.

Steve DeRosa—

Assistant Chief of Department, Chief of the City of New York Fire Academy. We were both firemen in Ladder 102 until he got promoted out of there to lieutenant. As a chief officer, he had more than his share of spectacular fires. As a battalion chief in the 9th Battalion, he was the first chief on the scene of what would eventually be a tenth alarm for an eight-story piano factory on Forty-Third Street between Tenth and Eleventh avenues, the night of January 23, 1985. Chief DeRosa saw the fill cap blow off the fill pipe to three thousand gallons of fuel oil that was being vaporized from the fire and heat in the vicinity of the oil tanks in the cellar. Fourteen men, including a couple from Rescue 1, would probably have been killed if he hadn't observed this. They were ordered out of the cellar and within thirty seconds, fire blew out the front and rear. Chief DeRosa gives a good account of this "Manhattan Spectacular" in *WNYF* Magazine, in the second issue of 1985.

Joe Ippolito—

Deputy Chief, the captain who brought me to Ladder 102. A fine captain and a gentleman of the first order. Nobody wanted to disappoint him.

Al Donchin—

Fire buff of Engine 230 since World War II and photographer. His book of photographs, "First Due," depicts firefighting in Williamsburg and Bedford-Stuyvesant, Brooklyn in the FDNY's busiest years, 1959 to 1979. He was a smart, lively gentleman with a wonderful vocabulary.

Nicholas J. Rocko—

Al Donchin gave him credit for being a historian. Who would know better than Al?

John Gill—

Fire buff of Rescue 1 and good friend. He was a World War II Navy fighter pilot and FBI man in the New York Office. He is proud of having been a fireman in college and before entering the Navy.

Jackie Boyle—

Fireman in Rescue 1. Former paratrooper. Golden Gloves boxer. My friend of 30 years, since our Ladder 102 days. We figuratively and literally see eye to eye. A confident gentleman. If you were in trouble, you would want this tough man coming to get you. Extremely efficient and effective.

Bobby Burns—

"Brooklyn Bobby." Formerly of Ladder 112, Brooklyn. Fireman/chauffeur in Rescue 1 for more than 20 years. The son of a fire captain.

A fast-thinking fireman, great with tools. An extremely fine fireman, with no wasted motion—one of the best who ever walked through the door.

John Cerato—

"The Prince." Captain of Rescue 1, lieutenant of Rescue 1, fireman in Ladder 112 in Brooklyn and Ladder 4, midtown Manhattan. The first fireman in Manhattan to introduce himself to me. He was a stonemason from a long line of stonemasons. John and Ray Downey developed the FDNY Rescue Collapse Program.

Steve Casani—

Lieutenant Rescue 1, was brought to Rescue 1 by Captain Bill Anderson, who also brought me to the rescue company. He is the son of a chief. I told him that his father was my hero because he was a fireman for 20 years before studying and going through the ranks to battalion chief. Steve came from Ladder 12 in Manhattan as a young fireman. He was promoted young to lieutenant. He was assigned as a lieutenant to Rescue 3, the Bronx Rescue, and came back to Rescue 1 as a lieutenant to spend many years there. A respected officer.

Bill Anderson—

"The Black Swede." "The Captain." A barrel-chested former Marine of the Korean War, he had been a fireman in Rescue 1. A tenacious bull of a man with the temperament of a gentleman. In his other life, he was a plasterer who did fancy plaster-molding work in many mansions in upstate New York.

Tom Baldwin—

Captain of Rescue 1, as well as a lieutenant and fireman there. Born in Ireland and deeply religious, he was tall and angular with the strength to be the carpenter he was. He had high energy and was everywhere at a fire. You worked very hard with him, but it was always like working with your favorite uncle. It was said that they should have left him a fireman and paid him as a deputy chief. A wonderful, pure man. His son Paul retired from Rescue 1 just before September 11, 2001. It probably saved his life. Tom's son Joe is a fire officer and friend.

Paul Geidel—

Lieutenant in Rescue 1. Great with tools and everything else. One of those people who is good at everything. He was a legendary windmill pitcher in softball and played all over the country until he was 70 years old. He got his three sons to become Eagle Scouts. Gary and Mike became valued members of Rescue 1. Paul qualified me with the Lyle Rescue Gun, which is part of the logo of "The Rescue."

*Gary Geidel—

Fireman in Rescue 1. I knew and liked his brother Mike since he was a probationary fireman and for the following 20 years. I knew Gary later, after he came to Rescue 1 from Ladder 11 in the Lower East Side of Manhattan. I went to High Angle Rescue School with Gary and got to know him. He was a big handsome man and a gentleman. Like his father and brother Mike, he was good at everything. A tough former Marine. An Eagle Scout, killed at the World Trade Center along with the other men of Rescue 1 on September 11, 2001.

*Pat O'Keefe—

My neighbor and friend for 20 years. I knew Pat when he went to Ladder 35 after the Fire Academy and for many years before he came to Rescue 1. I had the pleasure to work with this beautiful man. Pat went through knee operations and fought to stay in the job. He was killed at the World Trade Center along with the other men of Rescue 1. He was an affable, handsome man. A cabinet-maker who loved sailing.

*Pat Brown—

Captain of Ladder 3. Lieutenant at 69 Engine. Fireman in Ladder 26, Rescue 1, and Rescue 2. A highly decorated hero of the FDNY. Pat was a boxer who sparred with boxing champion Roberto Duran. He was a Vietnam War Marine Corps veteran. Handsome, quiet, and soft-spoken. He would bring some beautiful young ladies to the firehouse to introduce them to us. I don't doubt that Pat and his men were with people in need of help at the World Trade Center on September 11, 2001, and for a man like Pat and the others, it was impossible to run and leave them. He was killed that day with the rest of the men of Ladder 3. He was a good friend.

*Harvey Harrell—

Lieutenant in Rescue 5. An eager and enthusiastic fireman as a member of Rescue 1. We went to many fires and emergencies together. Harvey and his brother, also a lieutenant, were both killed at the World Trade Center on September 11, 2001.

**Ray Brown—

Lieutenant in Ladder 113, Brooklyn. Fireman at Rescue 1. Ray was a former high school wrestler and football player. A big, handsome, cool-headed man who was very similar in nature and looks to his father, Ray Sr., who was also a fireman and lieutenant in Rescue 1 and eventually a deputy chief in charge of Special Operations Command (SOC), of which all five rescue companies are part. Ray was buried and badly wounded when the towers came down on September 11, 2001. He is one of the few survivors.

Hank Gonzalez—

Fireman in Rescue 1 and Squad 3 and Tactical Control Unit 731. A long-time friend. His brother Marty and I were friends and fellow gymnasts in the old Boys' High School. The brothers were both cool guys and former paratroopers. Hank was well-built and a great wrist wrestler. He spoke up for me at Rescue 1 when I indicated I wanted to go there.

Tony Limberg—
Lieutenant and fireman in Rescue 1. Lieutenant in Rescue 3. We have been friends since our Brooklyn days when he was in Ladder 119 and I was in Ladder 102. A big, powerful man who is articulate and a great piano man. Along with Hank Gonzalez, he spoke up for me at Rescue 1. A very fine, good man.

Jimmy Curran—
Lieutenant in Rescue 1. Jimmy came to Rescue 1 from Rescue 4 as a fireman. I worked with him as a fireman and as a lieutenant in Rescue 1. Later, we would both be lieutenants in Special Projects at the Fire Academy. This would be the forerunner of the wonderful Rescue School that exists today. Our desks faced each other and we were good partners. Whenever or wherever I worked with Jimmy, I knew that no matter what happened, it was going to be an interesting and fun day. He was affable and comfortable in all situations. He had a calming effect on those around him. He was charming and disarming. He was a great president of the Burn Center Foundation because of his innovative ideas at promotion. He would run art shows and have expert guest speakers on collapse of burning buildings, such as deputy chiefs Vinny Dunn and Ray Downey. He once ran a promotion and retirement party on the aircraft carrier museum, the Intrepid. He told the people in charge that it would be around 300 people and it turned out to be 1,500 people. He backed up his ideas with his own total commitment and action. We were together at the Waldbaum's fire. Our son George had the honor of singing at Jimmy's funeral.

*Ray Downey—
Deputy chief, captain of Rescue 2. One of the leading authorities on collapse of burning buildings in the world. His sons, Joe and

Chuck, are now both battalion chiefs. Joe was a college wrestler and Chuck was a college football player. Ray developed the Rescue Collapse Program for the FDNY, along with Captain John Cerato of Rescue 1. Ironically, Ray Downey would be killed in the collapse of the World Trade Center on September 11, 2001.

George McGann—

Captain of Ladder 25. Lieutenant in Ladder 26-2. Fireman in Ladder 44 and Rescue 1. As a captain, he sent some of his best men to Rescue 1. Quick-thinking and smart, he is a good judge of men. A very engaging and enjoyable person to be around.

Hugh McGloin—

Captain of Ladder 21, fireman in Rescue 1, came from Engine 58 and Ladder 26 Harlem. On January 23, 1985, a 10-alarm fire in an eight-story mill-constructed piano factory caused it to collapse onto the 1894 firehouse and home of Rescue 1. The middle of Rescue 1's three-story brownstone firehouse was completely caved in. At the time, Battalion Chief Steven DeRosa wrote a great account of this spectacular fire, which appeared in *WNYF Magazine* in the second issue published in 1985. *WNYF* (With New York Firefighters) is the quarterly magazine of the FDNY. Rescue 1 was without a home. As Deputy Chief Ray Brown, formerly of Rescue 1, said, "The Rescue are like good hunting dogs. They are good in the field, but don't bring them into the house." Captain Hugh McGloin of Ladder 21 gave us a home for four years while our firehouse was being rebuilt. It was a good marriage for everyone. Hugh McGloin is smart and articulate.

Paul Hashagen—

Fireman from Ladder 25 to Rescue 1. An all-around valued member of Rescue 1. Highly decorated and very good at everything, including firefighting, diving, and high angle rescue techniques. A hockey player. An author of "The Rescue Company" and other books. A talented artist/cartoonist who signed his work "Hash."

*Ronnie Bucca—

Fireman in Rescue 1. Fire Marshal, FDNY. A paratrooper and helicopter door gunner in Vietnam. Joe Angelini would dub Ronnie, "the only man in Rescue 1 to earn his wings," as a result of surviving a five-story fall. With a broken back and half a year spent in a body cast, Ronnie fought his way back to work in a year. He had a parallel career in the Special Forces Reserves as a Military Intelligence Warrant Officer. An expert on terrorism who foresaw the kind of attack that occurred at the World Trade Center on September 11, 2001. In the late 1980s, he was the first person I ever heard mention a second attack on first responders. A marathon runner who made it up to the 78th floor of the South Tower. He was killed on that day when the building collapsed. He is a subject of the book on Muslim terrorism, "A Thousand Years for Revenge."

*Joe Angelini—

Fireman in Rescue 1. A good and pure, religious man who did 40 years as a fireman in FDNY. We were both gymnasts and he once displayed a strength move called the flag on the vertical handbar at the rear of the Rescue 1 apparatus, while we were doing 40 mph. I had the honor to eulogize Joe at his funeral. Joe and his son, Joe Jr. of Ladder 4, were both killed at the World Trade Center on September 11, 2001. He was a cool, fearless, God-fearing man.

John Dowd—

Fireman in Engine 230 and Ladder 108. My good friend in our Engine 230 years. He went to Ladder 108, while I went to Ladder 102. He is a funny man with a great sense of the ridiculous. He could make me laugh.

Tom Ianelli—

Came to Engine 230 after seven years in the NYPD. He was a champion handball player of whom it was said, "If he had the serve, you were finished." A *bon vivant* who didn't know how to cook until he got in the FDNY, he achieved "Chef" status in the firehouse with his gourmet meals. Tom, Hank Zuercher, and I once rode bicycles 160 miles in a day. The three of us walked 50 miles to see if we could do it, then we did it again at another time just for fun. Another person who just was good at everything he did.

John Driscoll—

Senior fireman in Rescue 1, a.k.a. "Sergeant Major." Aggressive on the fire ground. The "Celtic Warrior."

Paul Schmidt—

Lieutenant in Ladder 9. Fireman in Rescue 1. A college wrestler who might have made the U.S. Olympic team if he hadn't been ill. He once was the Wrist Wrestling Champion of the World in Las Vegas. Angular and powerful, an impressive man.

Pietro "Pete" Valenzano—

Battalion chief and head of Special Projects at the FDNY Fire Academy. He was serious about any job he took on. Under him, we trained all the truck companies of the FDNY in the use of Maxi Air Bags and the Hurst tool (the Jaws of Life), along with extrication from auto accidents. He was a fine man who was loyal to those who worked for him.

Bill Riley—

The senior man in Rescue 1. Six foot two inches tall and powerful. He was "Mr. Riley." A very imposing man, but at the same time, a gentleman by choice. He and I were in groups 2 and 3 for 14 years and I can still see his big back trudging up the stairs in front of me. A rock of a man who loved history. All of our sons were impressed when they met "Mr. Riley" at Rescue 1's quarters. At age 12, Leif, seeing aerial ladders raised at a fire on Ninth Avenue said, "Dad, the firemen are big, but Mr. Riley is really big."

John O'Rourke—

Chief of Department and Commissioner. The former captain of Ladder 114, Brooklyn. This charismatic man always had an entourage of firemen around him. A handsome, down-to-earth Irishman with the ability to tell great stories. He was as comfortable with the troops as he was with the top. This charming man remembered everyone's name. I will never forget the brightness of his presence.

Freddy Zarilli—

Captain in Ladder 1. Fireman in Ladder 4. Big, powerful, and highly humorous. He would tell young fireman Donny Solacito that when they got into a job to "move fast, especially if the rescue is coming in, because they are always right on your ass." Donny would eventually go to Rescue 1. Freddy was smart and one of the best bow-hunters I have ever known. He is my good friend.

The Rescue 1 Study Group for Lieutenant FDNY:

**Al Fuentes—

Captain of the Marine Division, lieutenant in Rescue 2, fireman in Rescue 1, the "spark plug" for the study group and a very sharing man. Buried when the towers of the World Trade Center collapsed, he was rescued from his entrapment 20 minutes from what would have been his death. Originally listed as dead, his being alive was one of the few bright spots on that day. I always said, "Al had to be descended from conquistadors."

Barry (Finbar) Meade—

Captain. Lieutenant in Ladder 120. Fireman in Ladder 11 and Rescue 1. A tall, handsome gentleman with high enthusiasm. An alert and lively man. An ocean-sailing captain. An ocean lifeguard and member of his college rowing team. An unpretentious, athletic man. He helped make studying bearable.

Bill Bessman—

Lieutenant. Fireman in Rescue 1 for more than 20 years. A six foot four inch college and Army basketball player who was impressive to see in fire gear. He looked like a tall, lean giant. He was my idea of the "Thinking Truckman." A very effective fireman. He should have been a chief. His imitation of an Italian racing driver with wrap around sunglasses and an accent would double me over and still brings a smile to my face.

John McAllister—

Lieutenant in Rescue 1. Fireman and chauffeur in Rescue 1 for more than 20 years. He came from Ladder 103, Brownsville, Brooklyn. A smart, funny man who always managed to get where the action was. In the two years we all studied together, his wife Carol almost died three times. She encouraged him to stay with it, but it took its toll on him. He barely hung in there, but he made it. His two sons, John and Joe, became firemen and officers.

George R. Kreuscher—

Lieutenant in 42nd Battalion, Brooklyn. New York City Fire Academy Instructor to Probationary Firefighters. Special Projects Instructor in FDNY Collapse of Buildings Program, Confined Space and Accident Extrication. Fireman in Engine 230, Ladder 102, Williamsburg, Bedford-Stuyvesant, Brooklyn and Rescue 1, Manhattan.

Our Firemen Sons:

George P. Kreuscher—
Our oldest son. Third-generation fireman. Former Marine and wrestler, assigned to Engine 93, Washington Heights, Manhattan. A victim of a molotov cocktail thrown at the fire apparatus while responding to an emergency during a riot. After time in the Burn Center and a year of rehabilitation, he spent the next five years in Ladder 44, Morris Avenue, the Bronx, fighting to stay in the job he loved and wanted all his life. With 10 years in the FDNY, he had to leave. It may have saved his life on September 11, 2001.

Leif Kreuscher—
Our youngest son, who has spent the last 10 years in Engine Company 209 and Ladder Company 102, Bedford-Stuyvesant, Williamsburg, Brooklyn. He is now a veteran himself, with his time alone. His time at the World Trade Center, one hour after the towers came down on September 11, 2001, has changed him forever. He is a third-generation fireman. Through the night of January 23, 1985, he accompanied me to the tenth-alarm fire for an eight-story piano factory building on Forty-Third Street between Tenth and Eleventh avenues. The collapse of the piano factory destroyed the quarters of Rescue Company 1, located next door. He was 12 years old and five feet tall; today he is a powerful six feet tall and a veteran fireman. Living 50 miles away from the World Trade Center may have saved his life. After hearing of the attack and calling Mary Lou and me, he had to drive the 50 miles, arriving there just after the towers collapsed, instead of just before.

The Rescue School that exists today in the FDNY is the result of the men of the Collapse Rescue, Rescue 3 in the Bronx, who helped in establishing it when it was part of Special Projects.

They were: Lieutenants John Norman and Mike Weinlein, who would both become assistant chiefs. Lieutenant Jerry Murtha, Rescue 3, and firefighters of Rescue 3 John O'Connell, Conrad Tinney, Harry Christiansen, John Hopkins (now a captain), *Ray Meisenheimer, *Chris Blackwell, Davey Dangerfield, and Danny McDonough. Firefighter Stan Sussina, Rescue 3, and firefighter Tim Kelly, Rescue 1 (later a lieutenant in Rescue 4), were very helpful in establishing "High Angle Rescue" with mountain-climbing techniques and confined space rescue techniques in the FDNY.

Dignity, decency, intelligence, self-motivation, dedication, and bravery without measure are virtues common to everyone on this very incomplete list. In 31 years in the FDNY, "The Men" never ceased to leave me in awe.

* *Killed on September 11, 2001, at the World Trade Center*
** *Wounded and survived the collapse of the World Trade Center towers on September 11, 2001*

Epilogue

The most impressive thing to me about the Fire Department New York has always been the extraordinary men who do the job—dedicated and heroic sometimes beyond belief. For many years, I have wanted to write something that would somehow convey what it is to be a firefighter and what it was when we were called firemen.

Today, there are women in the fire department and they work hard to do a good job. Women were introduced to the fire department late in my career so I had very limited exposure to women of the fire service. The couple that I knew, I liked. However, my training and forming were done by men who were called firemen. Firefighter is the modern title for the profession and that is the way it is now. My experiences were, on the whole, with the men called firemen. That was the way it was then. Today, many people still use the terms firefighter and fireman interchangeably.

It would be impossible to put into a single volume the varied and wonderful men I knew. The selection system that brings people to the fire service is such that it does a very good job of getting the caliber of people that will do such a dangerous and often dirty job. The personalities are as varied as any other group of people. However, there is a quality of confidence that a person must have in order to choose this profession. It is not for the faint of heart. That is the common thread.

Whatever a person thinks it is to be a firefighter, it is really an unknown until he or she is one. That comes long after training, with the experience of actually being on the fire ground. There is no way of imagining the dark, hot, and dangerous world a firefighter lives and survives in and sometimes dies in. It is not all gloom though, mainly because of the high spirits and sense of humor that many have. Early on, firefighters develop a sense of mortality that gives them a deeper appreciation of life. I would say that most are better people for having been in the fire service than they would have been had they not been there.

As a captain friend of mine once said, "The job is so obvious that if you didn't do it, you wouldn't be worth a damn." That is true, so the brave act is signing on and the rest just goes with the job. Still, in a job where it is expected that you will be brave, there are acts of selflessness and bravery that leave even the brave amazed.

The beautiful fire trucks and engines that are kept that way because they are expensive and so essential are important pieces of equipment. The various tools that are carried on the rigs enable the rescue of people from every calamity imaginable. But it is always "the men."

These frantic words, "Someone is still in there," "My baby is in there," "There are kids on the sixth floor rear" will send firefighters scrambling toward where the victims are with or without hoselines. The aggressiveness and fast thinking that goes into gear upon such pleas is the extreme heart of what it is to be a fireman. There is no bravado. It is the total focus on the saving of a life or lives, regardless of whose they are. They are trapped, in deep trouble, and it is the fireman who must get them.

At the World Trade Center on September 11, 2001, the firefighters that first arrived knew one thing for sure. People up there were in trouble and they would have to do everything to get to them. Subsequent fire companies coming in from Upper Manhattan and Brooklyn would all commit to the aid and rescue of those trapped. All five rescue companies of the FDNY from all five boroughs would also respond to this unimaginable toll of human misery and entrapment. All the men of the rescue companies would die that day, along with all the others. The supreme sacrifice of devotion.

When movies are made about urban firefighting, in order to have something to show on the screen, the glow of fire gives visibility to the scene. In reality, in most cases, the fire ground inside is smoky, hot, and dark, like James Joyce's description of hell, "Heat with no light." Heat that is often almost unbearable to unbearable.

In small areas or apartments, searches are made singly or in pairs rather quickly. Large areas like large stores and warehouses are done by whole companies, working off search lines, which takes more time. There is no magic to rescue. It is working your way toward those trapped under the most terrible conditions, with great exposure to yourself. However, great satisfaction comes with knowing you may have saved a life directly or indirectly.

Often, it isn't possible to rescue people at fires without getting water on the fire. This requires engine companies to crawl on hands and knees or even on their stomachs, in order to get into areas that are 500° at a point halfway to the ceiling and around 1000° at the ceiling. This is done to get to the heart of the fire in order to extinguish it thoroughly. This is a nasty business and enginemen take a beating doing it. Given New York City's population density, more lives are saved by this aggressive attack with charged hoselines than any other way. Enginemen are the grunts, the unsung heroes of the FDNY. They are the first company a chief wants to see come on the scene at a fire. An engineman is wet most of the time, no matter the outside temperature.

The first company to which I was assigned, in the summer of 1964, was Engine Company 230. They were in the top 25 busiest engine companies in New York City. Located on Park Avenue in Williamsburg, Brooklyn, they also responded deep into Bedford-Stuyvesant. They were a respected and busy outfit with a lot of senior men, many World War II veterans among them. These guys knew their duty and they were the men who broke me in. My whole attitude toward the job was formed here, by these men.

Captain John Blondell of Engine Company 230 had been a flight engineer on B-17s in the Eighth Air Force out of England and over Germany. He was a serious and aggressive leader. He would finish his career as a deputy chief—a strong first captain.

Lieutenant John Wakie, a tough bull of a man who had been promoted out of Ladder 102, was always the truckman looking for another way. He had high standards for himself and made me want to measure up. I talked about him so much at home that my oldest son George, as a little boy, thought it was "Wakie's firehouse." He would eventually become the captain of Ladder 108 and, after that, a battalion chief. A most wonderful man. A great ball player.

Lieutenant Ed Whalen, a study partner of John Wakie's, was also promoted out of Ladder 102. Tall, lean, handsome, and a former college basketball player for Long Island University. He was the epitome of what it was to be a fireman in looks and bearing. He had a wonderful sense of humanity that made him what he was. A very fine man who would become the captain of Ladder 112 and eventually a battalion chief.

Gentleman Jim Licausi, Captain Blondell's chauffeur/motor pump operator, was a senior man. He took me under his wing and showed me how smooth and dignified a fireman could be—a great example to a young fireman as to how to conduct himself.

Dom Chiaravalle, who would later become a lieutenant, could speak four languages: French, Italian, German, and English. He was an interrogator's interpreter in the Army Counter Intelligence Corps at the end of World War II. Extremely charming with a great silver tongue and a great amount to say in a way that made you want to hear it. Exuberant and smart, he could fill a room by himself.

Bill Reid was a good friend of Dom Chiaravalle's and equally charming. Bill was a World War II Marine with an extraordinary sense of humor and a unique outlook on life. I don't think he ever looked up to or down at anybody in his life. A totally self-actualized man, both dominant and confident, with an ability to talk to the lowest- or highest-born person. He was a big powerful man with a loud cackle of a laugh that would get me to come from any other part of the firehouse to hear what he was laughing about, which was often the absurdity of current events on which he had the most humorous point of view. Bill and Dom could be seated at the table of a king and I am sure they would have had him rolling off his chair. God, they were smart, funny men.

Then there was Frank Truochio, "The Truocha." Frank also was a funny man and a World War II veteran. He once told me that when he saw the Japanese railroads at the end of the war, he found it hard to believe that the Japanese had had the audacity to take on America. Frank was successful in the stock market and was very free and sharing to all of us with his knowledge. Frank took dancing lessons on the G.I. bill. He taught me how to tango in the kitchen of Engine 230. In fact, Lieutenant Danny Nastro, who was coming into the kitchen, did a mock about face when he saw us.

There were many more wonderful men who became my friends in Engine 230, who taught me many things, but most of all, what it was to be a member of a fire company in the City of New York.

My memories of morning coffee around the table in the back room kitchen of Engine 230 with the off going and on coming shifts of men with the accompanying banter and laughter are with me always. My whole attitude toward the job I loved was formed there by these lively, colorful, brave men.

Responding to approximately twenty-eight thousand alarms in 31 years, with about a third of these being fires, another third being emergencies, with the final third as false alarms, there were too many circumstances to enumerate. It would be a daunting task to mention all the wonderful people I worked and lived with over the years. Because we usually write about the highlights or unusual events, there are literally thousands of heroic acts that go unmentioned or are overlooked. I had the fortune to know and see many people of every rank in action. Only a few are mentioned and those not mentioned were only due to the circumstances of not being there at the incidents described. I am a fortunate man and privileged to have known so many heroic men.

Appendix

George R. Kreuscher, Lieutenant, F.D.N.Y., Retired

Appointed To:
Fire Department New York: May 23, 1964

Promoted To:
Lieutenant: August 25, 1990

Assigned To:
Engine Company 230 (1964–1969) Williamsburg/Bedford Stuyvesant, Brooklyn
Ladder Company 102 (1969–1974) Williamsburg/Bedford Stuyvesant, Brooklyn
Rescue Company 1 (1974–1990) Manhattan
Battalion 42 (1990–1995) South Brooklyn

Detailed To:
New York City Fire Academy as an instructor (1990–1995)

Certifications:
New York State Emergency Medical Technician & Instructor (1975)
Diver—Blackwater Search & Rescue/Commercial Divers Institute NAUI (1983)
New York State Fire Behavior and Arson Awareness (1990)
National Fire Academy Building Construction (1990)

Educational Methodology (1990)
New York State Accident Victim Extrication Instructor (1992)
F.D.N.Y. Collapse/Building Construction and Stabilization Instructor (1992)
F.D.N.Y. Confined Space Rescue; Vertical Removal Instructor (1993)
F.D.N.Y. Collapse/Interior Shoring Instructor (1992)
F.D.N.Y. Collapse/Void Access and Victim Removal Instructor (1993)
F.D.N.Y. Collapse/Exterior Shoring Instructor (1993)
University of Maryland Confined Space Entry and Rescue (1993)
ROCO Corporation High Angle, Structural and Confined Space Rescue I & II (1994)
New York State Confined Space Rescue Instructor (1994)

Education:
Nassau Community College A.A.S./Respiratory Therapy (1972)

Responsibilities:
Active Full Duty Fire Officer
Instructor of F.D.N.Y. Probationary Firefighters
Instructor in Special Projects/Instructed Active Fire Companies in the use of Cutting Torches, Hurst tool/Extrication, Air Bags and all other Special Rescue Tools
Assisted in development of Collapse of Buildings training for all five F.D.N.Y. Rescue Companies & Support Trucks
Instructed in Collapse overview, Interior Shoring, Exterior shoring, Void Exploration, Confined Space Rescue and Building construction related to collapse
Assisted and Coordinated the development of the auto accident extrication program that trained over 6,000 F.D.N.Y. firefighters and officers
Represented F.D.N.Y. at National Safety Council Symposium in Chicago—regarding the training and equipment used by F.D.N.Y. in confined space rescue
Public Speaking at other city agencies, Police Dept., Bridge & Tunnel Authority
Master of Ceremonies at Fire Prevention Week Ceremonies at South Street Seaport and Rockerfeller Center